TYING THE Forever KNOT

My Journey to Understanding Marriage's Greatest Hurdles

My Journey to Understanding
Marriage's Greatest Hurdles

Dr. Cedric D. Alford

Copyright @ 2023 by Dr. Cedric D. Alford

All rights reserved. No part of this publication may be reproduced, distributed, or transmitted in any form or by any means, including photocopying, recording, electronic or mechanical methods, without the prior written permission of the publisher, except in the case of brief quotations embodied in critical reviews and certain other noncommercial uses permitted by copyright law.

This publication is provided "as is", without warranty of any kind, express or implied, including but not limited to the warranties of merchantability, fitness for a particular purpose, or non-infringement.

While Dr. Cedric D. Alford has made every effort to ensure the accuracy and completeness of information contained in this book, neither TheDrCed Leadership Development LLC nor the author assumes any responsibility for errors, inaccuracies, omissions, or any inconsistency herein. Any slights of people, places, or organizations are unintentional.

ISBN: Paperback 978-0-9971448-2-6

Published by TheDrCed Leadership Development LLC

Book layout and cover design by Olga Pomazanova
Photo on the cover: unsplash.com

For information regarding permission requests, write to:
Dr. Cedric D. Alford, MBA

TheDrCed Leadership Development LLC
P.O. Box 616, Rowlett, Texas 75048-0616

Email: dralford@thedrced.com
Printed in the United States of America.

Dedication

This book is lovingly dedicated to my wife, Bonita; my children, Alexia and Tyler; my sister, Raschunda; and in memory of my late mother, Clara Aubrey Wright. To the couples beginning their marital adventure and those aspiring to fortify their bond: Your quest for understanding and enduring love epitomizes the depth of commitment. May this book provide clarity, wisdom, and inspiration on every step of your journey together.

If you find it in your heart to care for somebody else, you will have succeeded.

— *Maya Angelou*

Table of Contents

Dedication	5
PREFACE A Letter to the Readers	9
Acknowledgements	15
PROLOGUE The Top 10 Reasons Marriages Fail	17
CHAPTER 1 Lack of Communication	21
CHAPTER 2 Infidelity	41
CHAPTER 3 Financial Problems	59
CHAPTER 4 Growing Apart	77
CHAPTER 5 Lack of Intimacy and Emotional Connection	97
CHAPTER 6 Different Values and Goals	115
CHAPTER 7 Family Pressures	135
CHAPTER 8 Work and Career Pressures	157
CHAPTER 9 Mental Health Issues	177
CHAPTER 10 Lack of Effort	197
The Beginning of Our Journey Together	215
The F.O.R.E.V.E.R. W.E.D. Workbook for Couples	219
References	221

PREFACE

A Letter to the Readers

Dear Readers,

I am humbled that you've chosen to join me on this journey by opening these pages. If you picked up this book for guidance from an experienced marriage counselor or psychologist, let me be upfront: that's not my role. Yet, I firmly believe that our shared stories and experiences can be just as illuminating as any clinical analysis.

I'm Dr. Cedric Alford, a professor with an MBA and a doctorate in management specializing in organizational leadership. Leadership roles in prestigious organizations like Microsoft have enriched my professional journey. Of the 27 years of my career, I have been in a leadership role for 25. I have also been a graduate school professor for the past 15 years, teaching management, organizational leadership, strategy, marketing, and executive presence. I also led the marketing faculty for Jack Welch at his management institute. I have a published dissertation on women in technology leadership. But more importantly, my life's journey is that of an ordinary man who has faced and overcome many challenges.

Considering the management and leadership background I've shared, you may wonder why I would choose to write a book on marriage. Many have lauded the strength and beauty of my marriage to my wife Bonita and the exemplary upbringing of our children, Alexia and Tyler. Such accolades often left me contemplative, particularly considering the intricate journey Bonita and I have shared. Although our children were never the cause of concern, I've always been struck that rarely people delve into the "how" behind our story.

Take Tyler, for instance. Many admired his prowess on the football field, his skills on the basketball court, or his musical talent during symphonic performances. Yet few inquired about the countless hours he dedicated to practice or the identity of his private instructor. Today, they see Tyler as a well-spoken, worldly young man with degrees from Iowa State University. Still, they remain largely unaware of his journey, the challenges he faced, or even the humble beginnings from which he hailed.

Similarly, Alexia received praise for her volleyball skills and eloquence in debate class. Yet, rarely did anyone express curiosity about her private league experiences or her mentorship under Ms. Kaye, a force of nature who, before succumbing to cancer, instilled in Alexia a relentless drive for excellence. As she now carries the title of "Dr. Alexia," few probe into the tumultuous beginning of her academic journey.

When it comes to Bonita, many acknowledge her role as a dedicated stay-at-home mother and, later, her career transition to a Respiratory Therapist. However, the narrative usually ends there without delving deeper. Few are privy to the heart-wrenching episode when our son Tyler, at just 18 months, experienced a febrile seizure that nearly claimed his life – that pivotal moment reshaped our family dynamics. Having grown up working tirelessly in her father's fields, Bonita made the conscious and sacrificial decision to stay home. This allowed her to be a cornerstone for our family and transformed her into a beacon of support for many of our older friends. She became an indispensable aid, particularly to three friends battling cancer. As the only stay-at-home mom in our close-knit community, Bonita often took on the role of caretaker and driver. Tragically, two of those friends didn't make it.

It wasn't solely friends or distant acquaintances who noticed the strength of our familial bond. My relatives – nieces, nephews, aunts, uncles, and an expansive list of cousins – often remarked on our family's remarkable connection. One phrase from my aunts stands out: "Cedric, I am so proud of what you did with those kids." I would always fixate on the word "proud." To me, it signified more than mere recognition. It hinted at an understanding that I, or rather we, had surmounted significant obstacles. It seemed they were implying, "Considering your upbringing,

it's quite impressive how well your children turned out." And to be frank, given my tumultuous childhood, this observation wouldn't be off the mark.

As adults, my sister and I stand as pillars of our community, celebrated for our accomplishments and cherished families. I am a respected professor and former Global Director at Microsoft. In parallel, my sister shines brightly as Lieutenant Colonel Raschunda Aubrey of the U.S. Army. At face value, our trajectories are nothing short of remarkable.

But dig a little deeper, and a more complex tapestry unfolds. Our childhood was far from idyllic. Though our mother's love was undeniable, it was interspersed with episodes of abuse. As children, we naively attributed our harsh punishments to the normative discipline of that era. But as we grew older, the grim reality emerged: our mother grappled with profound mental health challenges. My sister bore the brunt of this tumult, compelling her to "run away" from home by the age of 15. Consequently, from the age of 13 until my high school graduation, I navigated our turbulent household alone, witnessing the manifold shades of our mother – her guilt and talent, her bouts of depression and moments of joy, and her deep-seated empathy.

These tumultuous years also bore witness to profound losses. The tragic death of my cousins Debra, Carl, and Tyrone to senseless violence, Roderick's heart-wrenching decision to end his life, Walter's battle with AIDS, and the untimely deaths of my friends Keith, Petey, and Fred, not to mention the violent end met by a dozen of my classmates.

My childhood and early adult life were marked by turbulence and uncertainty. Navigating those years, it took a significant portion of my marriage to truly believe I could open up completely without fearing losing the sanctuary Bonita and I built together.

Yet, life has its way of bringing silver linings. Amidst all my flaws and failures, I met Bonita who was nothing short of perfect for me. Our journey, too, was imperfect. Both of us lacked role models to show us how to raise kids in the suburbs or navigate the intricacies of married life. But we waded through, hand in hand, with love and patience as our guiding stars. We weren't perfect, but together, we became the best version of ourselves.

Our path together wasn't always smooth. From a daunting challenge on our wedding day that could have fractured our bond to a heart-wrenching incident 15 years later that left me a person with quadriplegia, Bonita stood as my unwavering pillar of strength. Her relentless love and commitment propelled us forward, even in the most trying times. It would be a glaring oversight to chronicle our journey without placing her at its heart. This book is, in essence, a tribute to her resilience and love as much as it is a testament to our shared experiences.

Our children, the pride of our lives, have also emerged from the cocoon of our collective growth. They've witnessed our evolution, challenges, and victories, charting their impressive paths in the process.

I must share that this book's essence isn't built on a pedestal of perfection but on the foundation of real-life experiences. The premise is simple: if someone with my background can find happiness in marriage and family life, so can you.

As we delve deeper into our journey, I hope you find solace in the lessons and stories shared, recognizing that the heart of this book is about accessibility. It's about understanding that we all deserve and can achieve a fulfilling marital and family life irrespective of our backgrounds.

These pages offer a unique blend of my academic research (as I am not a marriage counselor and had to learn the theory) and our journey. Each chapter commences with a business perspective – a domain I'm well-acquainted with. From there, I navigate the terrain of marriage, intertwining time-tested theories with the wisdom we've garnered over the years.

As a result of this book, I've also created something similar to the marriage concept– a workbook for those who lean on faith in their marital journey: *The*

F.O.R.E.V.E.R. W.E.D. Workbook for Couples. It encompasses the principles of Flexibility, Open Communication, Respect, Empathy, Vulnerability, Empowerment, Resilience, Wellness, Emotional Intelligence, and Devotion. Engage with it, and I hope it deepens your understanding and appreciation for the sacred bond of marriage.

This book 'Tying the FOREVER Knot' is as much a reflection of my journey as it invites you to reflect upon yours. Despite my imperfect start, my experiences in business and the intimate confines of family have crafted a story that I believe many can resonate with. I sincerely hope that our story serves as a testament to the fact that anything is possible with dedication, understanding, and love.

Thank you for joining me on this journey. I genuinely hope that, amidst my stories and insights, you find nuggets of wisdom that resonate with your life and relationship.

Warm regards,
Dr. Cedric Alford, MBA

Acknowledgements

Writing "Tying the Forever Knot: My Journey to Understanding Marriage's Greatest Hurdles" has been as much a personal introspection as an exploration. This exploration delves into the depths of my relationship and encompasses the myriad influences that crafted my perspective on commitment and partnership.

Central to this journey stands my wife, Bonita. Her support became the book's guiding light. While I tend to cherish our privacy, she discerned the transformative potential of sharing our story – a 25-year tale of imperfections and growth set against the backdrop of academic theory.

Two critical pillars shaped the essence of this book. Firstly, my late mother, Clara Aubrey Wright, whose struggles with relationships, mental health, and finances became invaluable life lessons for me. With time, reflection, and prayer, I have truly grasped her journey's intricacies and how they molded my view of marriage.

Then there is my sister, Raschunda Aubrey. Overcoming initial challenges with our mother, she emerged as an embodiment of resilience, retiring as a Lieutenant Colonel after a commendable 35-year military tenure. Her story, forever intertwined with mine, has played a pivotal role in shaping who I am today. Raschunda, I cherish the wisdom you have bestowed upon me and am honored to have you as my big sister.

To my children, Alexia and Tyler: While Bonita and I often receive praise for the wonderful individuals you've become, the truth is simpler. It is about keeping the dialogue open and evolving. You have gifted us countless lessons, and I sincerely wish we'd given you life-affirming values in return.

PROLOGUE

The Top 10 Reasons Marriages Fail

Marriage is not just a union but a journey of two souls evolving together, intertwined with moments of deep intimacy and daunting challenges. While some unions may falter, unraveling the 'whys' can pave the path to resolution and renewal. This book delves deep into the most common culprits behind marital breakdowns. Our sole goal is to arm you with insights and actionable advice, equipping couples to navigate these challenges and cultivate a flourishing relationship that stands the test of time. Here is what we will discuss:

1. **Lack of Communication:** Essential for marital success – effective communication allows partners to grasp each other's desires and perspectives. Its absence

fosters misunderstandings, conflicts, and emotional distance, often culminating in marital discord.

2. **Infidelity:** Infidelity is a grievous issue, profoundly damaging the marital bond. Such betrayals are often rooted in the absence of emotional and physical closeness, further jeopardizing the marriage.

3. **Money Problems:** Disputes over money and financial stress can severely strain marital ties. Such disputes might stem from varying spending habits, unequal earnings, or differing economic visions.

4. **Growing Apart:** As time passes, partners might evolve differently, leading to lost intimacy and connection. Such drift can complicate reconciling differences, contributing to marital dissolution.

5. **Lack of Intimacy and Emotional Connection:** The absence of physical and emotional closeness can evoke isolation and marital dissatisfaction. This growing gap can challenge the maintenance of a robust marital bond.

6. **Different Values and Goals:** Possessing differing values and goals can ignite conflicts and challenge marital collaboration. Disputes over core beliefs or aspirations can induce tension, risking marital stability.

7. **Family Pressures:** Familial interferences, unsolicited advice, or other stresses can stir conflicts within a marriage. These external pressures can weaken the marital bond, paving the way for its breakdown.

8. **Work and Career Pressures:** Career and work demands can strain marriages, especially when home responsibilities are neglected. This imbalance can breed resentment and dissatisfaction.

9. **Mental Health Issues:** Mental health challenges, like depression or anxiety, can impede maintaining a wholesome relationship. These can instigate stress

and behavioral shifts, making it arduous for partners to nurture a stable marriage.

10. **Lack of Effort:** Insufficient effort from one or both partners toward nurturing the relationship can jeopardize its survival. Navigating marital hurdles and preserving unity demands consistent dedication and commitment.

Throughout this book, we will explore these factors chapter-wise, providing in-depth research views, valuable insights and practical advice to help couples recognize the challenges within their marriage and overcome them, fostering a resilient and enduring bond.

CHAPTER 1

Lack of Communication

Bridging Gaps, Restoring Conversations

The warm glow of the restaurant's chandeliers cast a soft light on Sarah and Mike as they sat opposite each other, menus untouched. The live jazz band in the corner played a mellow tune, but an unmistakable silence lingered between them. They were celebrating their anniversary, which had evolved into "just a dinner" out.

Sarah's gaze drifted to a young couple two tables over, their fingers entwined, lost in whispered conversation and quiet laughter. She remembered when that was them: nights filled with stories, dreams, and shared secrets. She wondered about the occasion they were celebrating or if they just enjoyed having a date night.

"Mike," she began, her voice barely above the hum of background chatter, "when was the last time we really talked? Not about bills, or work, or the kids, or what is for dinner, but about us? About our dreams?"

Mike looked up, startled. The weight of her words dawned on him. "I...I don't know, Sarah. I guess we've been so busy."

But Sarah's eyes, shimmering with unshed tears, held deeper questions. Questions that had been pushed aside, buried under daily routines and responsibilities. "I feel like I'm losing you, losing us..." she whispered.

Mike reached across the table, touching her hand tentatively. "I feel it too," he admitted. "I miss us. I do."

The ambiance around them continued – couples engaged in conversation, waiters bustling about, the jazz band shifting to a more upbeat number. But for Sarah and Mike, time seemed to stand still as they confronted the widening chasm of their lack of communication, determined to bridge it before it grew any vaster.

Setting the Stage

Over the years, I have realized that marriage is an intricate dance, evolving with time. Both partners must consistently invest effort and show commitment. Just as in the case of Mike and Sarah, there are times in any marriage when communication becomes an issue. For those that yet have this to occur, my experience says, wait, as it is inevitable.

Despite the inherent challenges of fostering a resilient bond, various elements contribute to marital harmony. Prominently, effective communication stands out as a pivotal component. However, disconnect and frustration arise when this communication falters, potentially jeopardizing the marital bond. In this chapter, we delve into the significance of communication in ensuring marital success, understanding its intricacies, and strategizing to mitigate associated challenges.

Effective dialogue forms the heart of a union, especially in marriage, where two souls unite for a shared journey. This communication conduit allows couples to convey their emotions, desires, and apprehensions, facilitating mutual understanding. Within the sanctuary of a thriving marriage, couples can navigate even the trickiest subjects with openness and sincerity. This caliber of exchange cements trust and intimacy, laying a solid marital foundation.

Yet, many couples grapple with achieving this level of dialogue. A frequent stumbling block is the absence of active listening. In scenarios where one is not entirely present or engaged in a conversation, misinterpretations abound. Sometimes, one might sideline or downplay their partner's emotions, sowing seeds of discord and dissatisfaction.

As we venture deeper into the nuances of marital dynamics, communication emerges as a fundamental pillar. The vitality of any lasting partnership hinges on not just the message but its delivery. This chapter addresses how the lack of communication in a marriage can lead to failure.

Let us dive into the research first.

In-Depth Research Dive

According to Sprecher and Hendrick (2004), couples' satisfaction is directly linked to their perceptions of mutual communication patterns. Their research indicated that communication satisfaction predicted both love and overall relationship fulfillment. Positive communication patterns, characterized by understanding, validation, and empathy, were key elements of strong and enduring partnerships. They observed that couples who could discuss their heuristics (mental shortcuts to solve problems based on past experiences) and adapt their communication styles to their partner's needs demonstrated higher relationship stability and satisfaction over time.

The influence of early family experiences on marital communication is noteworthy. Feeney, Noller, and Callan (1994) explored the role of attachment styles on adult romantic relationships formed during early childhood experiences. Their findings revealed that individuals with insecure attachment styles – often developed from inconsistent or least emotional responsiveness from caregivers – had challenges in their romantic relationships. These challenges manifested as mistrust, fear of intimacy, and poor communication. Thus, understanding and addressing one's attachment style is crucial for fostering healthy communication in a marriage.

Research has shown that couples must navigate this new terrain carefully in digital communication, a modern twist to marital interactions. According to Ruppel, Jenkins, Griffin, and Tefertiller (2017), couples using digital means of communication, like texting or video calls, must establish rules and norms. These digital interactions can strengthen the bond if used appropriately, like sharing positive news and sending affirmations, or strain the relationship if used for conflict discussions or avoidance.

Doss, Simpson, and Christensen (2004) found that couples therapy could significantly improve relationship satisfaction. The study emphasized that early intervention is crucial. Couples who sought therapy during the early signs of communication problems were more likely to experience positive outcomes than those who delayed seeking help.

The dimension of empathy in marital communication has been underlined as paramount for sustaining connection. In a compelling study by Long, Angera, Carter, Nakamoto, and Kalso (1999), couples who underwent empathy training saw measurable improvements in their marital satisfaction. The training helped individuals learn to express understanding, validate their partner's feelings, and work on their emotional responsiveness, thus enhancing the quality of their interactions. It was concluded that empathy does not just involve understanding each other but it also extends to actively communicating that understanding to one's partner.

Conflicts, inevitable in any relationship, can either undermine or strengthen a marital bond, largely contingent on how they are managed. The research by Gottman and Levenson (1999) identified specific communication patterns that can predict divorce with alarming accuracy. Dr. John Gottman dubbed these the "Four Horsemen of the Apocalypse," these patterns include criticism, defensiveness, contempt, and stonewalling. The study emphasized that couples who replaced these negative patterns with positive communication behaviors, like humor and validation, dramatically improved the longevity and quality of their marriage.

Transitioning from the macro perspective of communication patterns to the micro intricacies, research has also emphasized the importance of "micro-moments" in marital interactions. According to Driver and Gottman (2004), these fleeting moments where spouses seek each other's attention and how they respond form the bedrock of emotional connection. Couples who consistently respond positively to their partner's bids for attention – even something as simple as acknowledging a comment about the weather – lay a foundation of trust, mutual respect, and intimacy.

Active listening, a subset of open communication, has been singled out as crucial for marital harmony. According to Weger, Castle Bell, Minei, and Robinson (2014), active listening is characterized by giving full attention to the speaker, refraining from interrupting, and providing feedback that demonstrates understanding. In their study, couples who practiced active listening reported fewer misunderstandings, reduced feelings of neglect, and an enhanced emotional bond. Notably, being genuinely heard and understood fostered a sense of validation and respect in the relationship, underscoring active listening as a foundational skill for couples wishing to strengthen their marital bond.

Active and passive listening are distinct communication strategies with implications and outcomes. A comprehensive study by Brownell (1990) underscores these differences by delving into the behaviors, attentiveness levels, and feedback methods associated with each approach. Active listening is characterized by the listener's full engagement in the conversation, demonstrated through behaviors like nodding, maintaining eye contact, and offering verbal acknowledgments such as "I understand" or "Tell me more." This type of listening demands that the speaker not only hears the words spoken but also comprehends, retains, and responds to the information, ensuring the other person feels valued and understood.

Conversely, as Nichols and Stevens (1957) detailed, passive listening is a more detached form of absorbing information. When passively listening, partners might hear the words spoken but may not fully engage with or interpret the underlying message. This form of listening lacks the feedback mechanisms in active listening and can often lead to misunderstandings or misconceptions. The partner's attention might drift, and they may miss key details or the emotional undertones of the conversation. Such an approach is less effortful but more detrimental than active listening as it can result in decreased comprehension and reduced rapport between partners.

Active listening requires the listener to focus on the speaker's words, ask clarifying questions, and sometimes provide feedback to demonstrate understanding. It involves concentration, empathy, and a willingness to understand the speaker's perspective. It is essential in building and maintaining healthy marriages because it allows partners to feel heard and understood, helping them resolve conflicts and build intimacy.

Reflections and Insights

A Pricey Problem:
The Domino Effect of Communication Breakdowns

In my early career at a prominent printing company, my role as the National Director of Database Marketing often put me at the crossroads of communication. We navigated large datasets to ensure the targeted marketing was precise and profitable. The mechanics seemed straightforward – organizations would share their customer data, and we'd identify the customers with the highest likelihood of responding, utilizing their budget information. This data became the foundation for the subsequent phase: creating the advertisement.

One particular campaign is etched in my memory for all the wrong reasons. An advertisement was crafted for a lawn mower priced at $399.99. However, due to a blatant miscommunication, the advertised price in print became $39.99. Despite the integrity of my team's data, someone overlooked several steps in the verification process. Before we could rectify the mistake, over 300 customers had availed of the erroneous offer, causing significant financial loss. Beyond this, the human toll was even steeper. Several team members downstream who failed in their oversight responsibilities ultimately found themselves without a job.

Let's draw a comparison here to the world of marriage and relationships.

In a relationship, the smallest missteps can lead to major setbacks. Imagine, for a moment, a couple preparing for a significant milestone – perhaps a surprise party for their child's landmark birthday. One partner believes they've agreed to host it at their home, thinking of an intimate gathering, while the other assumes they're booking a venue, envisioning a grand celebration. As the date nears, the partner expecting a great event discovers no reservations were made, while the other is overwhelmed with the sudden influx of guests in their space.

What would be the immediate outcome? It would be a stressful, hastily arranged party that neither envisioned, on top of that, draining both the energy and the resources. But the deeper consequence, much like the printing mishap, lies in the emotional aftermath: feelings of betrayal, frustration, and doubt.

The repercussions aren't just about a single event gone awry. It's about how one oversight can lead to eroded trust and potential long-term strains in the relationship.

Whether navigating team dynamics in the workplace or steering the course of marital life, the core lesson remains unaltered: communication is paramount. Overlooking details or operating on assumptions, no matter how minor they seem, can have repercussions that ripple far and wide.

Bridging Differences:
The Art and Challenge of Communication in Marriage

In the journey of marriage, communication stands as the sturdy bridge connecting the hearts and minds of two partners. As Bonita and I have walked this path together, the importance of genuine and transparent dialogue has become starkly evident.

It's easy to assume that communication is merely about talking. However, it's an intricate dance of verbal expressions, tone, and subtle gestures. A misstep can quickly spark defensiveness, derailing meaningful conversations. Such defensiveness can morph into a blame cycle, where instead of collaboratively seeking solutions, one partner pins faults on the other.

With more than half of my life by 2023 dedicated to our marriage, my life's experiences are deeply interwoven with Bonita. I'm grateful we've refrained from letting past disagreements overshadow our current conversations, which is extremely important for maintaining healthy communication between partners. Yet, the innate human tendency, known as "heuristics," can sometimes cloud our interactions.

Heuristics guide our brains in rapid decision-making but can be a double-edged sword during sensitive conversations. There's a risk of past grievances resurfacing, veering us away from the issue. Moreover, these mental shortcuts can lead us to draw premature conclusions, bypass essential information, or inadvertently belittle our partner's feelings, creating fissures in understanding. Therefore, the challenge is to sidestep these inherent cognitive pitfalls and hone the art of active listening.

True listening demands an effort, especially when one partner consents to the other. It's about forging a space where both partners' viewpoints find acknowledgment and validation, leading to decisions that truly resonate with both.

The rich tapestries of our backgrounds also characterize our union. Thanks to her father, Bonita's upbringing was painted with unity, commitment, and persistence. Despite life's intricate challenges, he was a beacon of strength, molding her concept of a resilient family.

On the flip side, my childhood was marked by absence and familial challenges. The sporadic presence of my father, juxtaposed with the internal conflicts of my home, left lasting imprints. Yet, amidst this turbulence, there were oases of joy and connection with my cousins, which bolstered my faith in familial bonds.

These varied upbringings meant that Bonita and I occasionally viewed scenarios through different prisms. But rather than letting these differences chisel gaps between us, they've been instrumental in forging a stronger bond. By embracing these differences and addressing them with open conversations, empathy, and mutual respect, we've merged our unique experiences.

The ramifications of a communication breakdown, especially in a relationship as profound as marriage, are multifaceted. Beyond immediate disagreements, it sows the seeds of mistrust, resentment, and doubt. By recognizing this and proactively addressing it, couples can navigate their shared journey smoothly and enrich their bond.

Tuning In: The Transformative Power of Active Listening in Our Journey

Over time, I've recognized that true communication extends far beyond mere words. It encompasses the silent pauses, the quirk of an eyebrow, and the subtle tension in the air – all of which are messages themselves. This has taught me the importance of being attuned to what Bonita says and what she expresses silently. Both forms of communication are essential to our relationship, demanding continuous effort, understanding, and dedication to bridge any gaps.

Active listening becomes even more vital, and at times challenging, for couples immersed in demanding careers requiring a substantial decompression period post-work. Arriving home tired after an exhaustive day can make it tough to be fully present for your partner.

My role as a business executive had me frequently on the move, often culminating in unpredictable arrivals at Dallas/Fort Worth International Airport. Yet, amidst this unpredictability, one thing remained consistent: Bonita. Time and again, she'd be there, waiting for me, a steady pillar in the whirlwind of my travels. Those moments, her unwavering support during my chaotic schedule, became emblematic of our unyielding connection.

During those moments, Bonita would fill me in on everything I had missed – updates about the kids, family matters, shows, neighbors, and the never-ending stack of bills.

As we embarked on our 40-minute ride home, I would offer casual responses like "hmm" or "wow," but truthfully, my active listening was lacking. Instead, I was preoccupied with fighting off jet lag and mentally compiling a to-do list for my client.

Did I have any upcoming interviews for the technical team? How was our company's financial position? What were my children's schedules and grades like? How was my mother? Did my dog eat today? Are we prepared for our board meeting?

I did my best to focus on what Bonita was saying, but I underestimated how physically and mentally drained I was. And just as I drifted away, lost in my world, Bonita's voice would bring me back to the present conversation.

"So, are you going to come with me?" Bonita would inquire, her voice adopting a lower, more commanding tone that effortlessly cut through the jumble of my thoughts.

"I just shared our schedule and what we've been up to. You were not even listening," Bonita would say.

Normally, I would do my best to avoid her accurate observation by attempting to find any word from the previous 90 seconds of conversation that I could repeat to buy me more time to think. However, after some of these long business trips, I just gave up pretending that I heard everything she said.

"Go where?" I would say, clearly demonstrating that I was not actively listening.

"You were not even listening to me," Bonita often said, sounding more matter-of-fact than disappointed.

Trying to find some semblance of a fight, I often tried the "spray and pray" method to solve the problem.

"You mentioned Tyler's game, the PTA meeting, Lex's volleyball tournament, and the 3:00 service," I would say, seeking clarification.

"But which one is tomorrow?" Bonita would respond, her Socratic approach as a gentle reminder that my lack of active listening had been recognized.

Feeling defeated, I would swiftly surrender and admit, "Okay, tell me again?" It was a clear acknowledgment that I had lost the battle of active listening. I had been passive in my engagement rather than actively participating in the conversation.

Earlier in our relationship, this kind of scenario frustrated Bonita, as I later learned. Back then, I was unaware of the skills and approaches needed to focus on the special moments with Bonita. I had not realized at this point that many fathers drove themselves to the airport, and their wives did not prioritize picking them up.

As time passed, I asked occasionally, "OK, tell me again," during our drives. However, I made a conscious effort to show progress. In the earlier stages of my career, when email and texting started, distractions were often caused by my mind wandering mid-conversation. So, I could not blame it on the "adult pacifier" – my mobile phone.

As our marriage grew and evolved, so did technological advancements and the temptations of scattered focus. For our first 15 years together, I found myself juggling multiple responsibilities. I was running the analytic consulting division of one company and building my marketing and web development company simultaneously. On top of that, I was pursuing a doctorate in management, adding yet another layer of activity to my already busy life.

My point is that the longer you are married, the more distractions you will have. What I came to realize was that being present in the moment with Bonita wasn't just about putting away the devices or clearing my schedule. It was about making a conscious effort to prioritize our relationship above all else. It meant setting boundaries at work, scheduling uninterrupted quality time together, and genuinely tuning into what she was saying.

As such, actively listening is a goal and an intentional skill that all couples should seek to learn and prioritize. It's essential to remember that in the grand scheme of life, the moments we genuinely share with our loved ones will always be more valuable than any email, notification, or task on our to-do list. Prioritizing active listening in our relationships is not just a skill; it's a testament to the value we place on those we love.

Religion, Communication, and Partnership in Decision-Making

In both personal relationships and larger communities, religious traditions often shape the dynamics of communication and decision-making. While some religious tenets advocate for certain hierarchical roles within families, others emphasize mutual respect and equality. The diversity in interpretation and practice becomes especially evident when individuals from varying backgrounds share their experiences and perspectives. This was strikingly clear during a men's conference I attended some years ago.

The attendees at the conference discussed how they deal with conflict with their partners. I offered that Bonita and I worked not to attempt to resolve issues in the heat of the moment and certainly not in front of the kids. As the men around the room began sharing their experiences, I noticed that the higher they were in the church and more aligned to what they discussed as Biblical thinking, their approaches were more aggressive and confrontational than mine.

"If there is an issue, you address it immediately." Said one participant.

"The kids need to see how the parents disagree and resolve issues. I do it in front of my kids," said another.

"I bring it to the pastor and let him mediate," said yet another.

Religious beliefs, communication styles, and decision-making approaches are inextricably linked, as demonstrated in the diverse experiences shared during the men's conference. Open and collaborative communication, founded on mutual respect and understanding, paves the way for making informed decisions as partners. Drawing from our religious backgrounds, Bonita and I could have easily fallen into a hierarchical model of decision-making. However, our choice to prioritize partnership and equality transformed our communication dynamic.

In relationships, it's crucial to recognize that religious teachings can influence communication patterns. While some may emphasize immediate confrontation, others may advocate for a more reflective and meditative approach. And while some may involve external mediation, others prioritize resolving conflicts within the confines of the relationship.

But at the core of all these is the importance of open communication, especially in the realm of decision-making. For Bonita and me, our religious background provided a foundation, but our conscious choice to engage in partnership-driven communication informed our approach to making decisions. We believe that for a relationship to thrive, it's imperative to maintain a balance of power and voice. This approach not only strengthens our bond but also encourages a healthy model for our children, showing them that in the face of diversity and challenges, mutual respect and collaboration are key.

Behind Closed Doors: Fostering Unity in Family Decisions

In every marriage, there lies an intricate dance of communication, shared with the world and some reserved for the confines of the relationship. How decisions are reached, discussed, and communicated – especially in front of children – paints a telling picture of a couple's dynamics. Bonita and I have fostered a unique approach that balances transparency with discretion, all while ensuring our children perceive a united front.

For instance, when deciding on our next vacation, the conversation might unfold like this:

Bonita: "Where should we head for the kids' summer vacation?"

Me: "I haven't settled on a place. What's on your mind?"

Bonita: "I considered a cruise to Cozumel, but the kids seemed to want to return to Fort Lauderdale."

Me: "Alright. What if we combine both?"

Bonita: "That's a thought. We could fly into Fort Lauderdale and then sail from there."

Me: "Sounds good. Let me know the budget."

Later, Bonita tells the kids: "Daddy wants to go to Fort Lauderdale and then cruise to Cozumel!"

Kids: "Thanks, Daddy!"

Though I might seem to have the final say, the decision is heavily influenced by Bonita's insights. One key element in our communication is prioritizing different aspects of a decision: I often focus on the financials, while Bonita addresses logistical concerns. But the beauty of our dynamic is not in these individual roles but in our synchronized collaboration.

I've realized the importance of not centralizing decision-making. Side-lining Bonita would deny our family her astute problem-solving abilities. Our strategy is clearly defining our roles and always leaving room for open communication. The final word might rest with me when decisions hang in the balance, but the approach is invariably collaborative.

What's intriguing is how Bonita communicates decisions to our children. Sometimes, she might present her decision as coming from both of us or even just from me. Early in our marriage, I struggled with this, wanting our choices always to be seen as mutual. However, I came to understand her intent. By sometimes framing decisions as mine, particularly when I was away on business, she emphasized my presence and role in their lives, a way to bridge the physical gap.

Over time, I've realized that while our contributions might manifest differently, they're equally pivotal. Whether it's the day-to-day calls or shaping our family's future, our combined efforts create a familial harmony that's both resilient and united.

Evolving Conversations: The Continuous Dance of Marital Communication

Throughout our marriage, the contours of communication between Bonita and I have shifted, evolved, and transformed. Like a living entity, every marriage undergoes periods of change, and our relationship is no exception. And while I have dedicated effort toward honing my active listening skills, I've been humbled repeatedly by unintentional oversight.

Take, for instance, the recurring theme where Bonita, with remarkable clarity, recounts a previous conversation, emphasizing, "I mentioned that on this date." Often, I'd find myself at a loss, wrestling with memory but unable to retrieve the information I required. These moments aren't mere lapses but reminders that communication is a perpetual journey.

With our children maturing and venturing on their own, our family's communication dynamics inevitably transformed. While they lived under our roof, Bonita and I were always strategic about our discussions, ensuring the children saw the outcomes rather than the intricate details of decision-making. However, as empty nesters, the nature of our conversations with our children shifted.

They frequently reach out to Bonita for those cherished, elongated chats, filling her in on the minutiae of their lives. On the other hand, my interactions with them are often purpose-driven. They approach me when faced with dilemmas, seeking solutions. This difference in communication style is not a point of disagreement but rather a reflection of our distinct roles.

With her ever-present empathetic ear, Bonita becomes the repository of their daily adventures, concerns, and schedule. I value the summaries she provides, keeping me in the loop. I appreciate this system we've naturally evolved into; it ensures that even if I'm not directly involved in every conversation, I'm never out of touch. And it also gives our children the best of both worlds.

They know they have Bonita's attentive ear for their daily musings and my problem-solving understanding when they encounter hurdles. This cooperation in our roles is something both Bonita and I have embraced. It's fulfilling to know that our children have two distinct avenues for support, depending on their needs.

Our delineated roles have been beneficial, but they come with a set of challenges. For instance, being the designated problem solver doesn't exempt me from the responsibility of active listening. If I, in my role, overlook or misinterpret something Bonita shares from her interactions with the kids, we run the risk of gaps in our collective understanding. It's akin to hearing about mutual friends who've drifted apart without your knowledge. The surprise underscores the importance of constant communication.

Communication, on the surface, appears deceptively simple. However, beneath this cover lies a complex web of emotions, intentions, and unspoken words. Balancing these elements, especially within the evolving dynamics of a family, is both an art and a science. As Bonita and I have discovered over the years, the key is flexibility, understanding, and the mutual desire to stay connected, no matter the changes life brings.

Strategies for Improvement

Open dialogue is the lifeblood of any enduring marriage, a bridge between two souls that ensures they remain in sync. Effective communication isn't just about sharing words; it's about understanding emotions, desires, and aspirations. When this bridge falters, misunderstandings flourish, causing minor disagreements which transform into significant conflicts. Emotional distances widen, and shadows of doubt cast their gloom.

For couples to thrive, they must cultivate an environment where voices are heard, feelings are acknowledged, and perspectives are valued. Rekindling the art of meaningful conversation allows partners to navigate their shared journey with clarity, ensuring that the path ahead is walked together in unity and understanding.

Couples often fail in their relationships due to unaddressed communication issues. These can be based on misconceptions, unspoken expectations, or conflicts from differing communication styles. As a crucial part of any relationship, especially marriage, having strategies to navigate these problems can mean the difference between a lasting relationship and one that ends prematurely.

As part of my research and through lived experiences, the following is a list of strategies that can support your success in open communications for your marriage:

- **Enhance Emotional Intelligence:** Recognize and understand your and your partner's emotions. Emotional awareness can lead to more effective discussion responses (Brackett, Rivers, & Salovey, 2011).

- **Reframe Negative Thoughts:** Before reacting, pause and consider the assumptions you are making about your partner's intentions. This allows for clearer communication (Gottman & Silver, 2015).

- **Establish "No Blame" Conversations:** Instead of pointing fingers, focus on expressing feelings and needs without laying blame (Markman, Stanley, & Blumberg, 2010).

- **Set Communication Boundaries:** Designate specific times to discuss sensitive topics when both partners are calm and free from distractions (Johnson & Whiffen, 2003).

- **Regular check-in:** Beyond problem-solving, have routine conversations about the relationship's health and future goals (Finkel, Hui, Carswell, & Larson, 2014).

- **Seek Feedback:** An outside perspective can sometimes provide insights into how both partners communicate. Consider occasional couples therapy or workshops as a proactive measure (Doss, Simpson, & Christensen, 2004).

Reflective Prompts

Finally, here are three questions to ask yourself to help improve communication in your marriage:

1. **Active Listening:** Reflect on a recent conversation with your partner. Were there moments when your thoughts drifted, or you formulated responses instead of truly listening? Consider strategies, like summarizing your partner's words or asking open-ended questions, to enhance your active listening skills.

2. **Defensiveness:** Recall a time when a simple conversation escalated into a disagreement. Did defensiveness play a role in that escalation? Identify triggers that make you defensive and brainstorm ways to approach conversations more openly and receptively.

3. **Past's Shadow:** Reflect on your communication habits and identify patterns that might have roots in past experiences or relationships. How do these patterns impact your current relationship? Discussing these observations with a trusted confidante or therapist can help recognize and break these patterns, paving the way for healthier communication.

_____

_____

_____

_____

_____

CHAPTER 2

Infidelity

Upholding Loyalty, Nurturing Faithfulness

Amelia stared at the photograph for what seemed like an eternity. The image, taken just last month at a friend's party, showed James, her husband, laughing with a woman she did not recognize. Their closeness, the lingering touch on his arm, and the way their eyes met told a story Amelia had refused to see.

She recalled the late nights at work James had been claiming, the unfamiliar scent on his shirts, the way he avoided her gaze when she asked about his day. Deep down, she had sensed something was off but never wanted to admit it.

Turning as she heard the front door creak open, she saw James step inside, his face lighting up in a smile until he saw the photograph clutched in her hand. The air grew thick, and the room's temperature seemed to plummet.

"Amelia," he began, voice shaking, "It is not what you think."

The weight of betrayal pressed on her chest, making it hard to breathe. "Isn't it?" she whispered, tears streaming down her face. "You promised, James. You promised."

He sank onto the couch, burying his face in his hands. "I never meant for this to happen."

Amelia, torn between pain and anger, realized that it was not just the act of infidelity but the erosion of trust, intimacy, and shared moments that hurt the most. The journey ahead was filled with the unknown, whether toward reconciliation or parting.

Setting the Stage

The moment James uttered, "It is not what you think," it hinted at his awareness of Amelia's doubts about his commitment. Why else would James choose those particular words unless he sensed her suspicions?

Infidelity, often termed a marital transgression, stands out as a painful tear in the fabric of trust that binds a relationship. Venturing into the dynamics of cheating, one cannot help but observe that it is more than just a physical or emotional affair. Infidelity manifests deep-seated issues at its core, often tied to unvoiced expectations, unmet needs, or the longing for novelty and adventure. As couples weave their life stories together, they can sometimes drift apart, allowing spaces for transgressions to seep in.

Navigating the tumultuous waters of betrayal requires courage and understanding. Certain questions originate when someone cheats. What leads one partner to stray from the sanctity of marriage? Can this breach of trust be merely seen as an act of impulse, or does it resonate deeper, reflecting the chasms that have silently grown over time? And more critically, once the forbidden line is crossed, can the bond be mended and trust ever be regained?

Marriage is a daily choice to remain committed to one's partner, embracing every complexity that comes with it. It demands an understanding of desires, vulnerabilities, and emotional landscapes. But when infidelity casts its shadow, the very foundation of this choice is shaken. This chapter aims to delve into the intricate maze of betrayal, exploring its roots, impact, and paths to healing. As we unravel the threads of infidelity, we strive to offer insights into understanding its complexities, aiming to fortify the bond of marriage against its tempests.

But first, some research on the topic.

In-Depth Research Dive

If a partner's heuristic defines infidelity as morally wrong and unacceptable, they might interpret their partner's innocent actions as signs of betrayal. For instance, they may misconstrue their partner's innocent friendship as an extramarital affair without investigating further or gathering solid evidence. Such premature judgments can lead to serious misunderstandings, cause unnecessary conflicts, and strain the relationship (Finkel, Eastwick, & Reis, 2015).

Alternatively, suppose an individual who operates under the heuristics and considers infidelity a common occurrence. In that case, they might downplay its seriousness, leading to avoidance of confrontation even when there are tangible signs of infidelity. This passive approach can also harm the relationship, as trust and emotional intimacy may gradually erode, leaving a void of unresolved issues and suspicions (McNulty, Olson, Meltzer, & Shaffer, 2013).

In either scenario, heuristics can interfere with effective communication and problem-solving within a marriage, resulting in an environment where assumptions and biases overshadow open dialogue and understanding within a relationship (Gawronski, 2004). Thus, it becomes crucial for partners to be aware of their inherent biases and consciously work toward considering all relevant information and perspectives when dealing with sensitive matters like infidelity (Fiske & Taylor, 2013).

To navigate these choppy waters, couples must foster a safe space for open dialogue where feelings, worries, and viewpoints can be openly shared and mutually understood. This practice aids in establishing a strong foundation of trust and emotional intimacy, which are vital for a resilient relationship (Hendrick, 1988).

However, it is essential to note that while heuristics can contribute to conflict and misunderstanding, they also possess the potential for positive application. When we know these mental shortcuts and how they can skew our perceptions and interactions, we can use them to navigate potential pitfalls in our relationships more effectively (Evans & Stanovich, 2013).

Heuristics are not only seen in interpretations around infidelity. Johnson, Caughlin, and Huston (1999) emphasized that spouses often rely on cognitive shortcuts when assessing their partner's commitment to the relationship. These heuristics can range from evaluating their partner's time spent with friends to their level of engagement in household tasks. When such judgments are formed hastily without adequate communication, they can add to the cumulative strain on the relationship.

Further, while open communication is emphasized as a remedy, it is equally essential to ensure that this communication is constructive. According to Rusbult, Verette, Whitney, Slovik, and Lipkus (1991), negative communication patterns, particularly in response to perceived betrayals, can push partners further away and reduce the willingness to repair the relationship.

On the brighter side, understanding these cognitive biases provides couples with a roadmap to strengthen their bond. Couples can challenge these biases consciously, ensuring that baseless assumptions do not undermine the relationship.

Misinterpretations rooted in biases have longstanding implications on marital longevity. According to Rogge, Bradbury, Hahlweg, Engl, and Thurmaier (2006), marriages characterized by mistrust and constant misunderstanding face a heightened risk of divorce. The nature of such misunderstandings, especially when centered on sensitive topics like infidelity, can deeply fracture the emotional bond shared by couples.

Real or perceived infidelity has been consistently identified as a leading cause of marriage failure. Leeker and Carlozzi (2014) found that the emotional aftermath of infidelity – including betrayal, loss of trust, and shattered emotional intimacy – is a significant predictor of marital dissatisfaction. Even in cases where no actual infidelity occurs, mere suspicion can create challenging rifts.

One potential solution lies in couples therapy and counseling. According to Christensen, Atkins, Berns, Wheeler, Baucom, and Simpson (2004), intervention strategies that focus on enhancing communication, addressing underlying heuristics, and fostering mutual understanding can effectively prevent the breakdown of marriages. These strategies aim to fortify the relationship against unfounded suspicions and emotional turmoil.

Ultimately, the key lies in understanding how biases operate and how they can influence the perception of partner actions. Couples can create a more stable and trusting relationship foundation by addressing these perceptions.

Reflections and Insights

Infidelity in Corporate and Marital Realms

Trust is the backbone of both personal and professional relationships. The silent agreement is clear: with trust bestowed comes the expectation of loyalty. Yet, the lurking shadow of betrayal – whether in marital vows or business dealings – can deeply mar these relationships.

In the intricate dance of corporate leadership, a world I once inhabited as part of a triad leadership team, the sting of betrayal can arise in the most subtle yet impactful ways.

I recall a gut-wrenching instance when two of us were tasked with sidelining the third. Encrypted communications flew back and forth, secret discussions were held, and the looming weight of our decision became palpable. It wasn't just a shift in corporate dynamics; it resonated as a profound act of betrayal. The sidelined leader, with whom we had shared years of mutual goals and visions, must have felt the shattering of trust akin to the sting of infidelity.

However, this 'corporate infidelity' isn't just a matter of high-level leadership decisions. It can infiltrate various levels, threatening the integrity of organizations. For example, an employee discreetly manages a role or project with another entity while purportedly giving their full attention to their primary job. Such divided loyalties can be likened to the hurt in a personal relationship when a partner becomes emotionally or physically distant.

Furthermore, consider the act of disclosing confidential company information. While at a glance, this may seem like a simple breach of trust, the reasons behind such actions can be more nuanced. Sometimes, this isn't about monetary gains or business advancement but rather a bid to foster personal trust or establish a closer connection with someone outside the professional realm. For instance, an employee might share a trade secret with a friend or acquaintance, believing that the shared knowledge creates a bond or proves trustworthiness.

This dynamic closely resembles emotional infidelity in personal relationships. Just as one partner might confide in someone outside their relationship, seeking emotional connection or validation, an employee might disclose proprietary information to gain personal assurance or a sense of intimacy. While different in context, both actions are breaches of trust, highlighting the importance of loyalty and discretion in professional and personal spheres.

Infidelity shakes the bedrock of trust and commitment – every concealed rendezvous, hushed phone call, or discreet message chips away at the bond. And just as deceitful practices within a company can result in financial fallout, tarnished reputation, or a hostile work environment, in the same way, marital betrayals can spiral into emotional turmoil, communication breakdowns, or the agonizing dissolution of the union.

Whether it's the hallowed boardroom or the sanctity of marital vows, betrayal casts scars that linger. Both realms echo the importance of clarity, steadfastness, and unwavering fidelity in our shared journeys. In constructing businesses or building lives, the twin pillars of honesty and loyalty stand tall, emphasizing their irreplaceable value. And while these lessons resonate universally, they have a raw, personal dimension. Here's a chapter from my story, a direct experience with infidelity.

Crossing Lines: Betrayals in the Heart and the Halls

A year before meeting my future wife, I was navigating the tumultuous end of a relationship fraught with infidelity. The woman at the center of this storm was

Desdemona, the receptionist at the bus transit company, where I was the youngest bus operations planner. Our roles often intersected. Community engagement was pivotal in my capacity, and Desdemona played a key role in ensuring the clarity of communication regarding bus operation requests. While I was typically the go-to for citizens wishing to speak about bus operations, occasionally, certain queries required me to seek Desdemona's assistance for further clarification.

My visits to her desk were initially mundane. The former receptionist, who occupied the space before Desdemona, was a maternal presence who had been with the company for years. But as she retired, the role underwent a series of temporary fills through staffing agencies, leading to a revolving door of new faces. Then Desdemona arrived, infusing the position with her vibrancy and ambition.

Her entrance wasn't just limited to the company; she also made a striking entrance into my personal space. I was inexplicably drawn to her, curious to understand the woman beneath the professional facade. And as fate would have it, our professional interactions began hinting at a deeper connection.

But with Desdemona, things were rarely straightforward. A mere three days into our budding relationship, a frantic call from her pulled me into a whirlwind. She had had a fierce altercation, not at her home as I had believed, but at the house of her friend, Kim's mother. Following the argument, she had been evicted. Naturally concerned, I invited her to my apartment as a temporary refuge while she found her footing. My gesture, rooted in chivalry and a genuine desire to assist someone in distress, took a twist I hadn't anticipated.

Desdemona arrived with two children in tow, her life packed into scant belongings that hardly filled my car's back seat, revealing that she didn't possess a vehicle. The sight of her, tears streaming down her face, perplexed me. I was accustomed to the tough realities of the hood, where evictions were frequent and seldom elicited much emotion. Yet, Desdemona's grief was palpable, indicating that there was more to her story than met the eye.

A month into her stay, subtle shifts in Desdemona's behavior began to surface. She started borrowing my car under varying pretexts but developed a pattern of returning it much later than agreed upon. Her outward disregard for my generosity slowly eroded my goodwill, and this trend continued into the next month.

It was during this testing period that introspection beckoned. Desdemona's repeated oversteps brought to light her boundaries (or lack thereof) and forced me to confront my limitations. I recognized a significant flaw in my nature: a lack of assertiveness, particularly with women.

Growing up in one of the city's poorest areas presented its unique challenges. My humble surroundings often made me hesitant to invite potential partners to my home, a sentiment rooted in a young man's embarrassment rather than pride. This reluctance severely limited my dating opportunities, inadvertently leaving me inexperienced in navigating the dynamics of a committed relationship.

This backdrop made Desdemona's entrance into my life all the more significant. She was a new chapter, a departure from my past inhibitions. Yet, with her came challenges I had never encountered. My unfamiliarity with setting clear boundaries and confidently asserting a 'no' was exposed, leaving me vulnerable. Through her, I began to see the gaps in my understanding of relationships, prompting much self-examination about my past reservations and my envisioned future.

Tangled Trust: My Odyssey with Desdemona

I had never really learned to navigate disagreements with women. But one weekend, after a band performance, I realized the importance of addressing this issue. I knew I needed to confront the unhealthy situation that had taken root in my absence. I resolved to tackle it head-on upon my return.

Frustrated, I finally told her it was time to leave.

To my shock, she responded aggressively, claiming that I could not kick her out because she had put her name on my lease. In disbelief, I rushed to the apartment office only to discover that she had indeed registered herself and her children as residents, stating that she had been living with me for over 48 hours. That constituted a Common Law Marriage in Texas, leaving me in a tangled legal mess.

I painfully realized I had been manipulated by Desdemona, a 21-year-old with three children, having lost a fourth. I respect young parents – my grandmother had her first child at 13, and some strong women I know were mothers by high school graduation.

However, this situation was particularly complicated because each of Desdemona's children had a father who had served time in jail for domestic violence. Two of the three fathers were now out – all of this was new information for me.

Night after night, I agonized over her consistent delay in returning my car. She was using that time to go on dates with two of her children's fathers.

Her infidelity was revealed in a series of unexpected ways.

First, I met each of them, who paid child support and had visitation. These visits meant she would have them come to my apartment to pick up their child. Now that I was common-married and could not figure out how to get out of the relationship, Desdemona and I lived life as if our relationship were normal and we were married, except that we were not.

Around six months into our "arrangement," Desdemona returned to our apartment after leaving me alone with her kids for four hours. Concerned and curious, I asked her where she had been. Unexpectedly, her demeanor shifted into a state of intense rage. Her eyes turned red, veins bulged in her neck, and she spat out words, accusing me of doubting her and lacking trust.

In that heated moment, she confessed angrily that she had gone to the movies with her child's father. She insisted it was none of my business. To add salt to the wound, she revealed they had been intimate, leaving me hurt and disrespected.

Her actions, such as claiming a stake in the lease and engaging with her child's father, left me feeling betrayed and utterly perplexed. It took immense strength on my part to gather the courage to remove her from my apartment, even though it meant supporting her financially by providing a deposit for a new apartment and co-signing for a car – anything to get her out of my life.

Amidst the pain, I had a lingering ache – an irrational longing for her. Unexpectedly, I discovered a profound attachment to her two children as I became a consistent presence when she was absent.

While I was away from the city for a tour with a band, Desdemona contacted me. She expressed her longing and mentioned her children needed shoes. I told her I'd try to meet her that Sunday. I returned a day early, hoping to drop off the shoes. I knocked on the door several times, knowing she was there after seeing her car, the one I bought, outside. She eventually opened the door.

As I handed her the bag, I saw another man sitting in her living room, his shoes off. It was her second child's father – a stark reminder of her infidelity and our shattered trust. The weight of deception again bore heavily on my heart, leaving an indelible mark of pain and betrayal.

At that moment, her son's father sitting in her living room looked at me and said, "What's up, Ced?" I replied, looking him straight in the eyes, "Bro, I don't have a problem with you. Desdemona said your son needed shoes, and I thought she needed assistance."

"It is all good," I stated, dropping the bag with the shoes at her door and turning around to leave. In my view, that would be the last time I interacted with her. So, I thought.

As I walked away, her last words, "Damn," hung in the air. It seemed like she realized the game was over. But little did I know, the story was far from over.

Three weeks later, I parked my car in the employee garage, unaware of the brewing conflict with Desdemona. Meeting my coworker outside, we prepared to head to breakfast. He pointed to a familiar sight unfolding before us as we stood there.

"Ced, isn't that Desdemona?" he asked, oblivious to the turmoil she had caused. I turned and saw her stepping out of a car – again, my car, the one I had bought for her. But someone else was behind the wheel – yet another man who was not one of her kid's fathers.

At that moment, a wave of emotions crashed over me – betrayal, disbelief, and the sinking realization that our tangled connection was far from untangled.

My emotional intelligence shattered. I angrily confronted Desdemona at the entrance to the company where we both worked, demanding, "Who was driving the car I bought?"

Her bold response stoked my fury. "Why?" she taunted as if my sacrifices for her meant nothing.

Then, she delivered the ultimate blow. With a twisted smile, she admitted, "You know I've been messing around with your boy," referring to the person who had just dropped me off.

She was a stark contrast to any woman I had known. By 21, she had four children and a tumultuous personal life. Despite living with me, she continued intimate relationships with several men, including her children's fathers. Her commitment seemed fleeting, and her trust boundaries perplexing, as evidenced by allowing yet another man the privilege of using her car. The depth of her infidelities and the seeming ease with which she shifted loyalties left me questioning her morals and values.

Overwhelmed, I stormed to the elevator. I pressed the third floor, attempting to hold in my emotions until I reached my office. After closing the door, I called my sister's boyfriend, seeking solace. Tears streamed down my face, but they were not tears of disappointment. They were the tears of a young man facing an uncertain future as if tomorrow held a jail cell. My sister's boyfriend tried to console me, reminding me to stay composed and assuring me that I would be okay.

In the subsequent months, I hired two attorneys. One to defend against Desdemona's false accusations at work and another to address our common-law marital ties, given she'd added herself to my lease.

The final court session marked a pivotal moment. Desdemona's absence flooded me with relief. This tumultuous chapter closed, but the lessons from this relationship had just started to take shape.

Throughout our time together, I was frequently reminded of the fathers of Desdemona's children. They had grappled with domestic abuse accusations against her in the legal system. This gave me pause, making me grateful for my foundational values, which kept me from becoming another statistic.

From Shadows to Clarity: Lessons Learned from Deception

Navigating through my tumultuous relationship with Desdemona exposed me to trust, deception, and personal discovery complexities. While the anguish of betrayal left deep marks on my psyche, it paradoxically served as a compass, guiding me toward the personification of loyalty, commitment, and the many facets of faithfulness.

The branches of Desdemona's deceit extended beyond mere secret encounters or concealed rendezvous. They made me question the essence of trust. Betrayal, as I confronted, was not solely about the act but the interplay of secrecy, manipulation, and the resonating aftershocks of distrust. As I meandered through this, I was addressing her transgressions and confronting the specters of my past: entrenched notions of masculinity, memories of observed domestic strife, and the embedded patterns of handling discord.

The narrative could easily have painted Desdemona as the antagonist. However, diving deeper revealed layers. What roles did the fathers of her children play in their shared past? Was there a repetitive cycle of trauma, catching everyone in its wake? My reactions, too, held up a mirror to my fears and insecurities. The shadows of unjust men and aggressive resolutions (starting with my father) from my past loomed large, threatening to influence my response.

Yet, from these depths emerged insights. The real mettle of strength wasn't found in retaliatory gestures or muscular confrontations. True strength is manifested in restraint and the enlightened recognition that perpetuating anguish only begets more pain. The wise counsel from my sister's boyfriend was instrumental here, nudging me to view strength as a force of empathy and understanding rather than aggression.

The gaping wounds of betrayal posed another dilemma: healing. Their rawness menaced, promising long-term scars. It was in this stage that Bonita's role became paramount. With her steadfast support and wisdom, she unveiled the path to recovery. She showcased that forgiveness wasn't about endorsing deceit but an act of emancipating oneself from the chains of bitterness.

While steeped in deception, this chapter with Desdemona also served as a pivotal juncture in my life journey. It wasn't merely about the tangible betrayals but more about the introspection that ensued and the lessons learned. The understanding that trust, once fractured, may not revert to its pristine state but could morph into a stronger, scarred version.

When Bonita entered my life, the specter of Desdemona remained uncomfortably close, casting its shadow over the early years of our marriage. Yet, the adversities I faced with Desdemona became a backdrop, accentuating the genuine goodness and understanding that Bonita brought into our union. The contrast was stark.

Where Desdemona's memories triggered apprehension and uncertainty, Bonita's efforts emanated warmth, trust, and patience. The very toxicity I had previously endured allowed me to recognize and deeply value the solace Bonita offered. Her presence acted as a balm, gradually dissipating the unease evoked by memories, allowing me to reconcile with them and find peace.

The Legacy of Infidelity: Shadows of the Past

While fidelity is the cornerstone of a marriage, the specter of past infidelities, whether experienced directly or indirectly, can cast shadows on a relationship. It's imperative to grasp that these shadows aren't just from personal betrayals but can also stem from the infidelity witnessed in familial or close relationships. This indirect exposure can shape perceptions, expectations, and trust dynamics within a marriage, even when the partners themselves remain steadfastly committed to each other.

My own family's history is tainted by a series of such betrayals. After her divorce from my father, my mother often found herself involved with men who were perpetually "on the verge of leaving their wives." Strong women in my family, like my cousins, ended up single after taking a stand against their unfaithful husbands. My father's own indiscretions provided me with siblings close in age, and the perplexity of familial ties further compounded when he eventually wed the sister of my mother's brother's wife. This tapestry of deceptions shaped my understanding of trust and commitment.

Such experiences, especially during formative years, become internalized. They shape how one perceives love, trust, and commitment. Thus, it's vital for partners to openly discuss and recognize the influence of these past shadows. Understanding that the anxieties and fears stemming from prior indirect exposures to infidelity are valid is the first step towards addressing them.

Bonita and I realized the importance of this open discourse. Acknowledging the weight of the past, and understanding its bearing on our present, allowed us to fortify our bond. By addressing these ghosts of infidelity, whether directly experienced or inherited from our family narratives, we could preemptively counter their influence on our relationship. Such transparency not only strengthens the foundation but also reinforces the walls of the relationship, ensuring that past specters don't undermine the sanctity of the present bond.

Strategies for Improvement

Trust forms the foundation of every strong marriage, and infidelity severely jeopardizes that trust, creating profound cracks in the relationship's bedrock. Betrayals of this nature often originate from a deeper absence of emotional and physical closeness, a void that, when filled by another, magnifies the original distance between spouses. The act of infidelity becomes emblematic of deeper issues at play – unmet needs, neglected feelings, or unsaid grievances. It reflects underlying problems, often culminating in intensified hurt and mistrust.

Addressing and recovering from such breaches in trust requires couples to confront the act and the factors leading up to it, fostering an environment where both partners can rebuild their connection on a foundation of transparency, mutual understanding, and unwavering commitment. As couples journey toward healing, it's essential to remember that mending from infidelity is about forgiveness and compassion, restoring and revitalizing the marital bond.

The repercussions of trust breaches can spell the make-or-break moments for many marriages. To navigate these treacherous waters, consider the following evidence-backed strategies:

- **Transparency and Candor:** Upholding a transparent communication line precludes many misunderstandings and misconceptions, often warding off feelings that lead to infidelity (Johnson, 2007).

- **Reaffirm Commitment:** Regularly reiterating one's dedication can reinforce trust and deter potential indiscretions (Rusbult, Martz, & Agnew, 1998).

- **Forge Shared Aspirations:** Crafting shared life aspirations can galvanize trust and unity between partners (Finkel et al., 2016).

- **Effective Trust Repair:** Recognize and employ strategies for mending trust post-breach, including genuine remorse and accountability (Lewicki, Tomlinson, & Gillespie, 2006).

- **Cultural Sensitivity:** Acknowledging cultural variances in trust perceptions can safeguard against unintentional violations and misunderstandings (Fulmer & Gelfand, 2012).

- **Avoid Keeping Score**: Chronicling past errors can eat away trust. Instead, focus on the current and what lies ahead (Knee, Lonsbary, Canevello, & Patrick, 2005).

Reflective Prompts

Finally, here are three questions to ask yourself to help prevent infidelity in your marriage:

1. **Trust and Healing:** Consider moments when you felt vulnerable or insecure in your relationship. Were these moments tied to concerns about loyalty or past indiscretions? Identify strategies, such as regular check-ins or relationship counseling, to rebuild trust and heal wounds.

2. **Understanding Temptations:** Reflect on your understanding of fidelity. Are there moments when you felt tempted or noticed your partner might feel tempted? Acknowledge these feelings and consider the underlying needs or emotions driving them. How can you address these needs transparently and faithfully?

3. **Open Dialogue:** Consider how frequently you and your partner discuss boundaries, past hurts, and future expectations. How can you foster a safe space where you feel comfortable discussing sensitive topics, ensuring clarity, and building trust?

_____

_____

_____

_____

_____

CHAPTER 3

Financial Problems

Uniting Financial Goals and Dreams

Shenita sat at the kitchen table, carefully plotting out their monthly budget. Receipts, bills, and a calculator lay scattered before her. Each calculation only deepened the worry lines on her forehead.

As she was engrossed in her task, the roar of a car engine pierced the quiet afternoon. Moments later, Trey burst through the door, excitement on his face. "Babe, look outside!" he exclaimed.

Shenita did, her eyes widening as they landed on the brand-new sports car parked in their driveway. "Trey... What have you done? Did you buy a new car? Really?"

He grinned sheepishly, "Don't worry. I got a great deal on it! You know I always wanted one."

"But... we can't afford this now," Shenita whispered, the weight of their financial struggles pressing heavily on her chest.

Trey's excitement faltered, but he defended, "I've been working hard, Shenita. My dad always had a new car. I thought it was time for me to treat myself."

Shenita's voice trembled with a mix of anger and desperation. "Our priorities are the house mortgage, the kids' education, and our savings. I don't care what you dad had. It is about us and what we can afford, Trey! We had a plan!"

He looked away, guilt evident in his eyes. "I just... wanted something for myself."

She deeply breathed, "We need to make decisions together, Trey. It is not just about what you want individually, but what's best for our family."

The shiny car outside contrasted starkly with the tension inside. Both Shenita and Trey faced a realization: for their financial health and their marriage, mutual respect and joint decisions were imperative.

Setting the Stage

Often described as a tool or resource, money holds power beyond its tangible form. Financial dynamics are nuanced in marriage, impacting much more than the bank balance. As partners embark on their shared journey, they carry their financial assets, liabilities, and deeply ingrained beliefs, values, and attitudes toward money. When aligned, these beliefs can pave the way for prosperity and harmony. But when they clash, financial fissures emerge, threatening to destabilize the marital foundation.

While love might be the cornerstone of a relationship, navigating financial terrains requires a delicate balance of trust, communication, and shared goals. How do couples reconcile differing financial aspirations? How do they face the weight of debt or the anxiety of economic uncertainty? And amidst these challenges, how do they keep the flame of their bond alive, ensuring that money does not overshadow the values that brought them together in the first place?

Beyond the numbers and bank statements lies the emotional and psychological landscape of financial interactions in marriage. From power dynamics to hidden insecurities, money becomes a lens through which many underlying issues come into focus. This chapter delves into the financial fissures in marriage, shedding light on the pitfalls, the lessons, and the strategies to weave a mosaic of financial harmony.

As we journey through these pages, we aim to equip couples with the insights and tools to ensure that money strikes a harmonious note in the dance of love and commitment rather than a discordant one.

Let's start by examining the existing research on the matter.

In-Depth Research Dive

Financial issues in marriages can stem from many factors, including the difference in financial socialization and monetary values between partners. According to Dew and Dakin (2011), couples who experienced significant differences in their financial upbringing or held disparate financial values were more prone to conflicts. This incongruence often resulted in disputes as partners' inherent financial behaviors, based on their upbringing, collided. Thus, the early experiences and teachings surrounding money that individuals bring into their relationships play a significant role in financial disagreements within marriages.

Debt, especially when undisclosed, plays a significant role in marital conflict. According to Archuleta, Britt, Tonn, and Grable (2011), undisclosed debt, often termed "financial infidelity," has been linked to trust issues within marriages, like emotional or physical infidelity. Their study found that financial mistrust could diminish the quality of marital relationships and even lead to dissolution if not addressed appropriately. They argue transparency and open discussions about financial commitments and liabilities are crucial for marital harmony.

The role of external economic pressures, such as job loss or unexpected financial emergencies, can also profoundly impact marital relationships. Amato and Rogers (1997) noted that external financial strains, especially those unexpected, exacerbated interpersonal conflicts in marriages. They found that couples often displaced their economic frustrations onto other issues, creating a snowball effect of dissatisfaction and discontent. Hence, the resilience of the marital relationship is tested not just by internal financial disagreements but also by external economic pressures.

Financial management skills, or the lack thereof, significantly influence marital satisfaction. According to Britt, Hill, and Tibbetts (2016), couples that lacked basic financial literacy and management skills were more prone to making detrimental financial decisions, leading to increased financial stress and subsequent marital conflict. In this research, the importance of financial education, not just in managing assets and liabilities but also in understanding a partner's financial perspective, was highlighted as a key determinant of marital happiness.

A study by Papp, Cummings, and Goeke-Morey (2009) found a direct link between financial disagreements and the degradation of marital happiness over time. The researchers argued that financial conflicts are particularly corrosive because they are more recurrent, difficult to resolve, and carry deeper emotional significance than other disputes, such as chores or in-laws. This nature of financial disagreements means they often resurface and persist, leading to chronic marital stress and an overall decline in relationship satisfaction.

The dynamics of power and control in relationships also come to the forefront when financial issues arise. Financial imbalances, where one partner earns significantly more than the other, can sometimes lead to unequal power dynamics. According to Vogler, Lyonette, and Wiggins (2008), when one partner controls most financial resources, it can sometimes create a dependency dynamic. The partner with less financial contribution may feel less empowered to voice concerns or make decisions, fostering resentment and dissatisfaction.

The stress arising from financial issues also has the potential to diminish intimacy and emotional connection between partners. According to Donnelly (2016), couples under significant financial strain often report decreased levels of intimacy and closeness. The researcher posited that the constant tension and stress from financial disputes could shift couples' focus away from nurturing their emotional bond, making it challenging to maintain a deep emotional connection. Over time, the emotional distance can lead to feelings of isolation and estrangement, further complicating the marital relationship.

Children in the family can also bear the brunt of financial disagreements between partners. An extensive study by Conger, Conger, and Martin (2010) revealed that children in households with consistent financial strain and parental discord related to finances displayed higher levels of emotional distress and behavioral issues. Notably, the study found that it was not the objective financial hardships that affected the children per se but rather the parental conflicts stemming from these issues. Hence, financial disputes not only strain the marital bond but also have cascading effects on the overall family environment and well-being of children.

Reflections and Insights

Money Problems:
The Parallels between Organizations and Marriages

Financial challenges are universal, affecting both business entities and personal relationships alike. However, the nuances in how they manifest and are addressed can draw uncanny parallels between the corporate world and marital life. A look at my professional journey illustrates this.

During my career, I was entrusted with a hefty $5 million investment to spearhead an Internet development team, aiming to scale from a single CFO to over a hundred employees within half a year. As we expanded, nearing the 80-employee mark, market dynamics proved our ambition to be strenuous. We had to extend hefty packages to fuel our growth, sometimes offering high school graduates an unsustainable $200,000 annually. Though our endeavors did reap the rewards, like establishing Walmart's inaugural website, our financial runway dwindled rapidly. Our aspirational aim of going public met a head-on collision with the .com bubble burst, resulting in the painful decision of downsizing those 80 hardworking individuals.

A decade later, history echoed when another venture I helmed teetered on the brink of acquisition. A seemingly sure-shot deal, with visions of a lucrative financial future, fell apart at the eleventh hour due to an unforeseen merger. The anticipated financial windfall from the merger vaporized, leading to the heartbreaking decision to let go of 60 dedicated staff members.

Both instances painted a clear picture: While a grand financial goal lay at the end of the tunnel, the journey there was fraught with obstacles. In business, as is evident, many ventures falter due to financial limitations before actualizing their goals. Similarly, financial strains are among the leading causes of discord in marriage.

Just as companies necessitate a robust revenue strategy and positive cash flow to flourish, marriages demand financial transparency, mutual financial goals, and a shared understanding of spending and saving. Without a clear, agreed-upon path in both scenarios, the likelihood of 'running out of runway' is high.

A marriage, like a business, thrives on shared aspirations. Couples dream of buying homes, traveling, providing the best for their children, or ensuring a comfortable retirement. Similar to a company's milestones, these aspirations require a well-charted financial strategy. When these plans are derailed due to unforeseen expenses, debts, or other economic hardships, the strain mirrors that of an organization running out of funds.

However, a silver lining is drawn from lessons in both domains. Financial challenges, whether in a corporate setting or a marital one, don't inevitably spell doom. It's the alignment and resilience that matter. As future companies I was involved with learned to adapt, align, and mitigate financial pitfalls, marriages can evolve and strengthen through financial adversity.

Navigating Uncharted Financial Waters: The Meeting of Minds

Business degrees are commendable, and young professionals with a year or so of experience often carry them with pride. They represent years of hard work, determination, and the promise of a bright future. However, textbook knowledge and brief stints in the corporate realm might not wholly equip someone to steer the intricate ship of family finances. This is particularly true when you're not just thinking for yourself but also for your partner.

Reflecting on my journey, I realized that my academic journey and brief professional experiences were, at times, more of a decorative shield than a practical toolkit. I walked into my relationship with limited financial understanding and a scar on my record – a recent theft case from my college years. This scar was later removed, but I did not know that then.

Coupled with that was my poor credit history and a recently repossessed vehicle. So, while on the outside, it might've seemed like I was primed to handle financial decisions adeptly, the reality was a different story altogether. I was unprepared, not just in terms of managing finances but in the subtleties of shared decision-making and long-term planning that relationships demand.

Here's the nuance: Financial understanding is not just about personal management; it's about shared management. And sometimes, when both partners boast of exceptional financial prowess, it doesn't necessarily lead to seamless decisions. The duality of knowledge can breed competition, a silent tussle on whose strategy trumps. But relationships aren't boardrooms; the goal is mutual growth, not individual ascendancy.

Drawing from my professional experiences, I remember the sage words of a former board member who entrusted me with his company. He emphasized the beauty of risk-taking and noted that a poor decision was forgivable. Yet, committing the same mistake twice wasn't. It was a lesson about learning, adapting, and growing. I realized this philosophy also applied beautifully to managing family finances.

As my wife and I embarked on our shared financial journey, the road was anything but smooth. We both carried our own baggage, with mine being more apparent, yet we each faced our own set of challenges. However, the foundation of our journey was built on recognizing our limitations and learning from our missteps.

Stay with me as I peel back the layers of our financial journey, revealing not just the challenges but also the triumphs, lessons, and shared moments that defined our path.

Charting Unfamiliar Terrain:
The Ups and Downs of Our Financial Voyage

Growing up, neither Bonita nor I had the advantage of witnessing sound financial behaviors within our families. When we married in 1998, platforms like Google and Bing were not at our fingertips, leaving us without easy access to financial wisdom. This vacuum made our journey toward effective money management a challenging one. Yet, we firmly believe it's never too late to learn. With the resources available today, everyone has the chance to bolster their financial literacy and carve a more prosperous future.

The complexities of my financial upbringing are both stark and contradictory. Growing up, our family was enmeshed in the confines of a closed community where opportunities to break free were limited. Conversations about money and fiscal responsibility were strangely scarce in our household, even though we resided in subsidized housing where a grasp on income and budgeting was pivotal.

The paradox deepens when considering my mother's credentials: possessing two accounting certificates, she diligently provided tax services to those around us. Yet, the same hands that managed ledgers and tax forms for others rarely imparted financial wisdom within our home, as parents rarely discussed "adult topics" with their children. Consequently, my early understanding of finances became intrinsically skewed, shaped more by the prevailing norms of our community than by the knowledge that existed so close, yet so out of reach.

This oversight led to a significant blind spot in my understanding of money. Despite the undeniable importance of financial literacy in daily life, I grew up without its guidance. An omission that would eventually catch up with me.

In college, I confronted the stark realities of financial mismanagement. My academic journey began on a high note, with scholarships covering my expenses, allowing me to excel and even tutor my peers. Yet, as time passed, these scholarships diminished, covering only a fraction of my needs. To bridge the gap, I turned to loans.

At the start of each term, receiving lump sums from loans created an illusion of affluence. Enthused, I would buy or order my books, rent an apartment, and even secure a phone line. But my lack of financial literacy, rooted in my past, saw me fumble. I struggled with balancing a chequebook, leading to multiple overdrafts. Before the semester's end, I sold those same books, borrowed aged library editions, and relied on classmates' notes.

My decisions in college were often driven by personal comfort without understanding the long-term financial implications. For instance, I valued the privacy of having my room for personal space and music practice, as I was a keyboardist and member of a college jazz band. I did not fully grasp the financial burden this choice would entail, and inevitably, by mid-semester, I would be strapped for cash, grappling with food shortages.

Hiding these financial struggles became a challenge, especially for my then-girlfriend. Subtle hints of my predicament emerged, like the need to crash at a friend's place at the start of school or my conspicuous absence from the dining hall. This façade of stability weighed heavily on me, with the growing emotional distance threatening our bond. I felt trapped in my web of deceit, fearing the truth would shatter my image of being that cool guy who was also a musician from Dallas.

Walking to my eviction-threatened apartment, the constant concern was sourcing funds for food amidst a hectic campus life. During these moments of despair, the unattended books in the library seemed like an enticing opportunity. The profound hunger and desperation propelled me into thoughts I had never considered when I accepted the engineering scholarship. Memories of my childhood resurfaced, recalling those in my community who turned to theft out of sheer need.

The mounting pressures did not merely remain financial; they took a toll on my emotional well-being and sense of self-worth. The strain of constantly feeling hungry and unable to focus began affecting my academic performance. What had started as a promising college journey slowly transformed into a battle for survival and self-preservation by my junior year.

University support systems were available during this trying phase. However, my pride became a barrier. Afraid of judgment and the potential loss of face, I hesitated to reach out, even to close friends. The isolation I felt was palpable, each day seeming like a testament to my inadequacies. Deep down, I yearned for a listening ear, a shoulder to lean on, or a word of advice.

During one particularly challenging week, as hunger gnawed at me and desperation set in, I stumbled upon an unattended book in the campus library. Yielding to the overpowering urge for a reprieve, I chose to take it, hoping to sell it for some quick cash. This act went against every fiber of my moral upbringing and left me battling emotions.

The guilt was undeniable, and the sadness weighed heavy on my heart. I had let down not just myself but all those who believed in my potential seeing me as a beacon of hope and resilience. They had witnessed my journey, my struggles to overcome adversity, and reach the hallowed halls of college.

Yet, in stark contrast to this guilt, there was an undeniable, albeit fleeting, relief. I could afford to satiate my hunger for the first time in days. The sight of my replenished fridge, stocked with essentials, offered a paradoxical sense of accomplishment, even if the means to achieve it were questionable.

However, as I prepared my meal that evening, the reality of my actions began to sink in, leading me to question the true cost of such momentary gains.

Over the next few days, I could not shake the ease with which I had stolen the book, sold it, and managed to have food. The temptation grew stronger, and I made the unfortunate decision to repeat my actions, believing that I would not get caught this time and that I could have both money and food. It was a flawed mindset, driven by a misguided sense of connection to other students who seemed to live a life of routine – eating, attending classes, studying without hunger, and repeating the cycle.

A Wake-up Call

Amid my contemplation, a deep baritone voice interrupted my thoughts – a call that would soon bring unexpected consequences and force me to confront the reality of my actions.

"Hello, Cedric. This is Sergeant Johnson. I need to speak with you regarding a book reported stolen a few days ago. You have two options: either come to my office today at the University Police Station, or I will personally come and escort you out of class."

The weight of his words hit me like a ton of bricks. I had been aware of the university's police officers, but an actual Police Station on campus had escaped my knowledge. Being a Black student on a predominantly White campus, the thought of walking around asking for directions to the Police Station sent a wave of unease through me. It was a situation I did not want to find myself in.

But here I was.

Reluctantly, I found and went to the Police Station to meet with Officer Johnson. Upon seeing me, he appeared surprised, as my name and voice on the voicemail had given him no indication of my race. Officer Johnson asked, "Son, we got a complaint from a student who said his book was stolen. After checking receipts at the store, we found your name. Did you steal the book?"

Feeling defeated, I bowed to authority and admitted, "Yes, sir. I took the book."

Officer Johnson raised his eyebrow, a mixture of disbelief and amusement in his eyes. "You signed your name on the receipt? Damn, you are a stupid ass."

I could feel the burning heat of embarrassment flushing my face as the weight of my actions settled upon me. Realizing how foolish and thoughtless my attempt at theft had been filled me with a deep sense of shame. It was clear to me now that a life of crime was not my path.

"I... I guess so...," I admitted, my voice laced with shame, my hand nervously rubbing the back of my neck. A complex mix of emotions washed over me – a blend of remorse for my actions and a strange relief that I had been caught.

Officer Johnson could not help but chuckle, though there was a hint of disbelief in his shaking head. He seemed genuinely curious as he asked, "Son, why the hell did you take the book?"

Taking a deep breath, I hesitated before mustering the courage to share my truth, "Sir, I was hungry. I came here on a full scholarship but struggled to afford meals when they raised the tuition. I have no meal plan. I tried to stretch my financial aid check but ran out of money after paying my rent. It was not enough. So, I did what I thought I had to do. I took the book and sold it back."

Officer Johnson shook his head, a mix of astonishment and empathy in his eyes as he responded, "So, you're here on an engineering scholarship, stealing books just to eat? Sounds like an excuse to me. Damn."

From Campus to Confinement

Before I knew it, the weight of my actions manifested physically. I felt the tight grip of handcuffs around my wrists, securing me to a chair. From that confined space,

I was transported, not in the company of friends or professors, but by University police, from the environs of academic halls to the stern walls of the county jail.

And then, there was the holding cell – a stark contrast to the freedom I had taken for granted just hours earlier. The cold, unforgiving light of the cell flickered, casting eerie shadows on the peeling paint and the iron bars that stood between me and the world outside. Those bars and walls now echoed the candid discussions and cautionary tales I'd heard in the neighborhood growing up.

The next four hours in that cell felt like an eternity. The gravity of realization weighs down every second. Here I was, worlds away from the lectures, libraries, and leisure of college life. An experience that served not just as punishment but as a profound lesson on choices and consequences.

The oppressive weight of my isolation was palpable. My mother, 200 miles away, was unreachable. She lacked both a phone and car; our only bridge of communication being the infrequent letters we exchanged.

My sister, potentially a lifeline, remained elusive, as I had failed to remember her new phone number in an era when phone numbers were committed to memory rather than stored digitally. She was active duty military at that time, so even if I was able to contact her, there was very little she could have done.

The thought of reaching out to my father was even more daunting. As a pastor, the implications of his son being caught stealing would be deeply distressing. Despite knowing of his past incarcerations, I aspired to be a different, better version. With trepidation, I dialed his number, tears streaming down my face. "I'm in jail for stealing. Can you help me?"

His response was an unexpected blow, "Son, stop crying and just sit it out." There was no offer of financial aid, no warmth or comforting words. His stance struck a sharp contrast to the tales I'd heard of him supporting prison ministries in his pastoral capacity. To others, he was a beacon of hope, but to his son, he advocated facing the consequences without reprieve.

Meanwhile, my peers went about their typical college routines – jotting down notes, engaging in academic discussions, and prepping for upcoming classes. They likely assumed I was right there with them, never imagining that miles away, I was confined to a stark, unwelcoming cell, waiting for my fate to be decided.

My salvation came in the form of a magistrate. Recognizing my lack of a prior record and the nature of my crime, he granted me a personal recognizance bond, sparing me any payment for release.

But even during such darkness, a glimmer of hope emerged. This grim reality provided a clarity I had never experienced before. It was, in every sense, a turning point. As the weight of my actions settled heavily upon me, I made a silent promise to myself: This would be the first and last time I would find myself in such a place. I would learn, grow, and rise above, ensuring that this painful detour would pave the way to a brighter future.

The book I had stolen had become an unintended symbol of my struggle, a reminder that I had lost my way in the pursuit of survival.

Money Problems: A Journey from Challenge to Growth

For a long time, I attributed my financial struggles in college entirely to the gnawing hunger and the desperate measures I took to appease it. However, as time unfolded and Bonita and I became more transparent with each other, I came to recognize my lack of financial understanding and stubborn resistance to seeking help as equally significant contributors to my hardships.

My financial challenges were not just occasional slip-ups; they were extreme, life-altering, and filled with hard lessons learned. Many might find aspects of my journey relatable, though its intensity might vary. Escaping a permanent record was a narrow miss, and its stark implications prompted a profound change in me. I was driven to recommit to personal integrity and financial literacy. I realized the value of a dollar and the heavy responsibility of managing it.

By sharing this, my aim is not to elicit sympathy but to shed light on the reality that was mine – a reality shaped by circumstances but transformed through acceptance and growth. Fast forward to today, and while I wear the badges of success, including three business degrees, the shadows of my past financial naiveté have a way of lingering, albeit positively.

When Bonita and I united in marriage, she did not just marry the man I had become; she married my history, experiences, and battles. And in the mosaic of our shared life, my early struggles with money management were threads that weaved their way in. We faced them together, learning and growing, reminding me that the journey to financial literacy is not a sprint but a marathon.

Not every couple will have our trip, but all couples can use open communication and partnership to set a solid foundation for their marriage based on their shared values and goals. It is a marathon best run with a committed partner by your side, showing that true love is not just about sharing joys but overcoming challenges together.

Strategies for Improvement

More than just a test of financial understanding, economic strains challenge the trust and teamwork foundational to marital harmony. Disagreements over spending habits, unequal earnings, or divergent financial visions can morph into disputes that overshadow love with worry and contention. Yet, money is a tool, and its management within marriage should ideally be a testament to shared goals, mutual respect, and joint future planning. As couples reframe their financial discussions from a lens of blame to one of collaborative vision-building, they empower themselves to transform monetary challenges into opportunities, crafting a shared economic dream underpinned by mutual understanding and shared responsibility.

By harnessing informed strategies, some of which are drawn from academic literature presented in this chapter, couples can bolster their financial bond and navigate around potential obstacles:

- **Unified Financial Vision:** Align shared financial aspirations early on, promoting mutual understanding and cooperation (Papp, Cummings, & Goeke-Morey, 2009).

- **Financial Literacy:** Equip oneself with budgeting, investing, and saving knowledge. Financial education decreases financial-related stress (Lusardi & Mitchell, 2014).

- **Open Money Dialogues:** Maintain consistent conversations about finances, removing the taboo often associated with money discussions (Dew, Britt, & Huston, 2012).

- **Set Clear Boundaries:** Establish thresholds for expenditures that require mutual decision-making, fostering a sense of shared financial stewardship (Archuleta, Britt, Tonn, & Grable, 2011).

- **Plan for Contingencies:** Constructing a contingency or emergency fund can reduce financial anxieties and disputes during unforeseen events (Kim & Garman, 2004).

- **Seek Financial Counseling:** Engage in a couple's financial counseling to provide structure and third-party insights into financial planning (Britt, Cumbie, & Bell, 2013).

Reflective Prompts

Finally, here are three questions to ask yourself to help deal with money issues in your marriage:

1. **Financial Values and Priorities:** Delve into your core beliefs about money. Are you a saver, spender, investor, or something else? How do these values align or clash with your partner's? Initiate conversations to understand and respect each other's financial philosophies.

2. **Setting Boundaries:** Recall financial disagreements arising from unplanned expenses or impulsive decisions. How can you both establish boundaries or guidelines for such situations? Would setting a budget or having regular financial check-ins be beneficial?

3. **Future Planning:** Envision your financial future together. Are there shared goals like buying a home, traveling, or saving for retirement? How do individual aspirations fit into this picture? Establishing a joint financial roadmap can help align your money-related ambitions and actions.

_____

_____

_____

_____

_____

CHAPTER 4

Growing Apart

Reconnecting Paths, Renewing Bonds

Michael sat on the porch, a Starbucks Grande Dark Roast Sumatra coffee warming his hands, watching the sun dip below the horizon. He remembered the days when Janelle would join him, the two of them weaving dreams about the future and reminiscing about their shared past. But those moments had become rarer with time.

Janelle, meanwhile, had found solace in her digital art studio, every creation a testament to her evolving passions. Her illustrations had transitioned from vibrant landscapes to abstracts, reflecting her changing self.

Michael missed the adventurous woman who dragged him on spontaneous road trips. He longed for the days when their interests intertwined seamlessly. Now, their weekends were divided between his hiking expeditions and her clients.

One evening, as Michael was flipping through an old photo album, Janelle walked in, her eyes drawn to a picture of their younger selves laughing carelessly on a beach. "I miss this time in our life," she whispered.

Michael looked up, his eyes echoing her sentiment. "We've grown and changed, haven't we?"

Janelle nodded, her fingers tracing the outlines of their younger selves. "But we grew apart."

"We can find our way back. I want to because I love you," Michael murmured, hope fading.

The silent room was filled with the weight of unsaid feelings and memories. While their paths had diverged, the journey of rediscovery beckoned, offering them a chance to realign their dreams and find shared ground again.

Setting the Stage

Change is an intrinsic part of the human experience, shaping our perspectives, aspirations, and identities over time. As individuals journey through life, they continuously evolve, adapting to new experiences, challenges, and self-discoveries. Within the intimate confines of a marriage, this journey of personal evolution takes on a dual dimension, where two parallel paths of growth are intertwined. Ideally, these paths meander harmoniously side by side. However, sometimes they diverge, leading partners in disparate directions. This phenomenon, commonly termed 'growing apart,' can subtly yet profoundly alter the dynamics of a relationship.

Couples often revel in shared dreams, interests, and aspirations at the dawn of marital bliss. Yet, as the years roll by, personal transformations can lead to shifts in values, goals, or passions. Sometimes, these shifts are complementary, enriching the relationship with new layers of depth. At other times, they introduce chasms of disconnect, where partners feel they no longer recognize the person beside them.

The intimacy once cherished might seem distant, replaced by an unsettling feeling of living with a stranger.

This chapter delves into the intricate maze of 'growing apart' in marriages. It seeks to understand the underlying factors that drive couples to distant corners of the relationship arena and the silent, often unnoticed, signs that signal such drifts. More importantly, it aims to guide couples on bridging these gaps, rekindle connections, and rediscover the love that might seem lost but often lingers beneath the surface.

In this exploration, we will navigate the delicate balance between personal growth and marital unity, striving to offer insights that help couples embrace change together, ensuring that their paths of evolution, while distinct, remain lovingly interconnected.

Before we delve deeper, let's review the research on this subject.

In-Depth Research Dive

The phenomenon of couples drifting apart, often termed relational disillusionment, has been the subject of extensive research. According to Stanley, Whitton, and Markman (2004), relational disillusionment is characterized by the gradual decrease in positive, affectionate feelings toward a partner, often replaced by ambivalence or negativity. This shift in perception is notably different from daily fluctuations in relationship satisfaction and can indicate deeper foundational cracks. The process usually involves couples moving from an initial stage of unity and passion to discord and disinterest, primarily due to unmet expectations or perceived differences.

Changes in each partner's interests and growth trajectories in a relationship can significantly contribute to drifting apart. Carstensen, Graff, Levenson, and Gottman (1996) highlighted the evolution of personal goals and values over time, especially when couples do not evolve synchronously. Their research elucidated that marriages face challenges when one partner undergoes significant personal growth or transformation while the other remains stagnant or moves in a different direction, leading to diverging paths and a lack of shared experiences.

Life stages play a pivotal role in marital dynamics. Parenthood, in particular, has been cited as a major transition that impacts marital satisfaction. According to Doss, Rhoades, Stanley, and Markman (2009), the arrival of the first child often results in significant shifts in marital satisfaction, with many couples reporting increased conflict and decreased intimacy. Similarly, the "empty nest" phase, characterized by children leaving home, presents another transitional period. Couples, having centered their lives around their children for years, may find themselves in unfamiliar territory, re-navigating their relationship without the immediate shared purpose of child-rearing.

Psychological changes, including the onset or exacerbation of mental health issues, also play a crucial role in couples drifting apart. According to Whisman (2007), partners suffering from mental disorders, notably depression or anxiety, often exhibit patterns of negative communication, reduced intimacy, and increased conflict. The partner's mental health affects their personal well-being and ripple effects on the relationship, creating an environment conducive to estrangement and relational disillusionment.

Relational disillusionment and ensuing marriage drift are closely linked with perceived and actual relational equity. Adams (1965) proposed that individuals assess relationship satisfaction based on comparing their contributions to the relationship versus the benefits they receive. Distress emerges when perceived inequity exists, especially when one partner feels over-benefited or under-benefited. In marriage, inequity can manifest in multiple emotional, financial, or task-oriented domains, such as household chores. Partners perceiving an imbalance in relational efforts might progressively detach, culminating in emotional drift.

While personal interests and life stages can create a chasm in marital relationships, effective communication has been repeatedly underscored as a crucial mediator. The study by Heavey, Layne, and Christensen (1993) highlighted that couples' inability to discuss differences in evolving interests could contribute more to relational drift than the diverging interests themselves. In many cases, couples often possess the capacity to tolerate diverging passions or pursuits, but the lack of open dialogue about these changes erect walls of misunderstanding and alienation.

One of the more insidious aspects of drifting apart is its silent and often unnoticed progression. Fincham and Linfield (1997) elucidated this phenomenon, noting that many couples misattribute early signs of detachment to temporal events, such as stress at work or temporary personal challenges. Over time, these initial dismissals can lead to an acceptance of reduced intimacy and connectedness as a new relational norm. This subtle, creeping nature of relational drift makes its detection and solution challenging, requiring proactive reflection and checks on the state of the relationship.

The importance of shared experiences in bridging the drift cannot be understated. Gable, Reis, Impett, and Asher (2004) posited that couples sharing positive experiences, or "capitalization," have better relationship outcomes. Such shared experiences, be it traveling, partaking in mutual hobbies, or merely reflecting on past positive memories, act as anchors, reinforcing emotional connectedness and serving as a buffer against the forces pulling couples apart. Ensuring a reservoir of shared positive memories and regularly creating new ones is a strategic approach to counteract the dynamics leading to couples drifting apart.

Reflections and Insights

Growing Apart in Organizations and Marriages: Navigating the Crossroads of Alignment

Life unfolds in seasons – professionally and personally. Relationships and roles transform as we journey through these seasons, often at contrasting rhythms. My tenure in diverse organizational environments has afforded me a unique perspective, illuminating a trend as evident in marital bonds as in professional relationships: the nuanced dance of drifting apart.

In my professional orbit, I've witnessed stellar leaders who, despite their dedication, found themselves on shaky grounds, battling the haunting question: "Where did it go wrong?" This sentiment mirrors the puzzlement in marriages where partners, lost in their daily lives, fail to discern the growing chasm between them.

Seeking clarity, when these leaders turned to me, my reflections often directed them inward. "At what point," I'd ask, "did you sense a shift in your role or importance?" Delving deeper invariably unearthed pivotal moments, instances where their contributions began to misalign with the organization's dynamic needs.

Regrettably, I've had to part ways with over 200 employees in my career. Though many of these departures were propelled by economic imperatives, a not-so-trivial set of employees echoed a more complex narrative. Discussions veered around macro business trajectories and intimate evaluations of fit and value. Decoding the "we're going in a different direction" often laid bare an underlying discord.

The corporate realm offers a vivid illustration: as organizations evolve, adopting new technologies, employees risk obsolescence if they don't adapt. Conversely, an employee might become so niche, so hyper-focused on avoiding turbulence that they fade into the backdrop becoming an afterthought in the company's grander vision.

Marriages, too, are vulnerable to similar divergences. Partners might find their once-shared passions fading, one embracing change and the other seeking solace in familiarity, widening the gap of shared aspirations.

Yet, this drift is a one-dimensional narrative neither in the office nor at home. Employees might sense a growing disconnect with a company's shifting ethos, just as a spouse might feel their union's foundational vows and visions wavering.

These parallel tales from boardrooms to living rooms echo a resonant truth: As growth and change are constants, alignment remains paramount. Whether in a corporate role or a marital bond, the onus is on individuals to periodically recalibrate, converse, and realign their trajectories. This conscious alignment is the cornerstone of lasting partnerships – whether sealed with a contract or a promise.

So, what can we do about this? The answer often lies in two things: communicate and adapt.

At work, it means having open conversations with your bosses and colleagues. Understand where the company is heading and see how you can fit into that picture. Maybe it's learning a new skill or taking on a different role.

In relationships, it's about checking in with each other. It's sitting on a quiet evening and discussing dreams, fears, and the future. It's about understanding and respecting each other's growth and finding ways to grow together, even if it means exploring new paths.

Staying Anchored:
The Power of Intentionality in Marriage

I always feared the notion of growing apart, so I took steps to avoid it actively. Our key value drivers from the beginning of our marriage were centered on being present in all aspects of our children's lives.

From the early days of diaper changes and helping with everyday tasks to never missing a game or event as they grew older, we made a conscious effort to be engaged parents. It was not always convenient or easy, but the joy and fulfillment we experienced were immeasurable.

Our children, Alexia and Tyler, have a seven-year age difference, which presented unique opportunities and challenges for us. It meant that Alexia would head off to college much earlier than Tyler. Initially, Bonita and I felt a tinge of sadness and loss, but we swiftly recognized that this allowed us to devote more quality time to Tyler and cater to his unique needs and interests.

We became intentional about attending his school and extracurricular events, trying to create family outings and engage in activities that brought us all joy. This shift in focus allowed us to embrace the present and strengthen our bond with Tyler during this phase of our family's journey.

Simultaneously, we faced the task of navigating the delicate balance between focusing on Alexia's high school and college journey and meeting Tyler's needs as he progressed through elementary and middle school. It was challenging to divide our attention and ensure that both children received the required support. I found it difficult to adapt to this change in dynamics.

Alexia's achievements made us proud, as her character and influence on others resonated deeper than any accolade.

Alexia faced a deeply challenging time during her senior year of high school and first year of college as she had to confront the heart-wrenching loss of my mother, one of her most cherished supporters. As a strong-willed young lady, the impact of losing her grandmother was evident in her college essays, where she contemplated the meaning of life and emphasized the significance of family bonds.

The loss affected her profoundly, as she not only mourned her grandmother's absence but also grappled with the changing dynamics in her relationships with her mother, brother, and myself. The daily connection, engagement, and problem-solving that once characterized our bond felt altered, creating a complex emotional landscape for Alexia to navigate during a crucial phase of her life.

In 2009, we prioritized regular trips to Ames, Iowa, where our daughter attended university, ensuring our family bond remained intact. Our visits to Ames were so frequent that local families and churches began to consider us one of their own.

Our involvement with the university increased in 2010 with Alexia's position as a Recruiting and Football Operations Student, supporting the then-head football coach Paul Rhoades program. She kept this role for years, eventually being hired by Matt Campbell's program for the same position and corralling his young kids on game day in alignment with the coach's wife.

Alexia's reputation and dependability across two ISU Football coaches afforded Bonita, Tyler, and me the privilege of game tickets and pre-game meals with the athletes' parents, provided we made the 600-mile journey – a challenge we willingly accepted for nearly every home game, driving or flying in from Dallas.

By 2016, when Tyler was contemplating his university choices, our deep involvement with Iowa State and Alexia's legacy became pivotal. Despite earning scholarships from various Big 12 schools, Tyler's bond with Alexia drew him to Iowa State. He followed in her academic footsteps and received the esteemed George Washington Carver Scholarship, the top honor awarded to the university's outstanding minority students.

Tyler's decision ensured our family's continued connection with Iowa and ourselves, as it allowed Bonita and me to keep our family together and not grow apart. We had already spent countless weekends there to support Alexia in her Ph.D. journey. Now, Tyler's choice amplified our commitment as he successfully auditioned for the prestigious Iowa State University Drumline, securing a position as a snare player.

Our trips to Iowa expanded to include cheering for Tyler during halftime shows as we embraced our dual roles as proud academic and band parents. We were also heartened to always stay with my daughter instead of a hotel. Alexia embraced those moments as well, as Tyler would come to her apartment making our family whole again. We would share in our dinner table ritual, albeit now at Alexia's table.

Our connection to the university strengthened further when Tyler transitioned from being a student and band member to taking on additional responsibilities. Channeling his longstanding athletic spirit, Tyler seized an opportunity to work as an equipment manager and practice assistant for the university's football team during his final two years of college. This decision allowed him to work closely with players like Alan Lazard, David Montgomery, and Breece Hall, who later made it to the NFL. Thus, our family's intertwining narrative with Iowa State University continued, marked by academic accomplishments, musical milestones, and athletic associations.

With our children now involved in football in their unique roles, it was an astonishing sight that evoked a sense of wonder. The distance between us, measured in hundreds of miles, could have been a deterrent. Yet, we invested time and resources into staying close as a family and partners.

Our decision was a conscious one. We understood the financial commitment these trips would entail. However, the investment was more than justified by assessing the immeasurable enrichment gained from fully savoring those 11 years of college life – the unforgettable memories, the shared victories and losses, and the moments of togetherness. When weighed against the value of these priceless experiences, every dollar spent represented an investment in our family's shared narrative.

Throughout our children's formative years and into their adult lives, Bonita and I discovered a formula that allowed us to stay connected and engaged. The true test of our ability to maintain that connection came after 2020 when Alexia and Tyler completed their education at Iowa State University. Alexia earned her Ph.D., while Tyler obtained three business degrees.

However, the pandemic disrupted our plans to visit Alexia as regularly as before. Tyler had settled in Dallas, while Alexia had embarked on her career as a professor, initially at Drake University, and after a year at Drake, the University of Arkansas actively recruited Alexia to become a professor. Now, residing in Fayetteville, the distance was reduced to a 5-hour drive, which was much more manageable than our previous 12-hour journeys.

During Tyler's time in Iowa, he met his future wife, Tegan. Tegan was a Division I athlete, playing soccer for Iowa State University after an illustrious high school career in Colorado. Understanding the importance of fostering strong relationships and serving as role models, Bonita, Alexia, and I consciously tried to include Tegan in every game, meal, and celebration during our trips to Iowa. After graduating from Iowa State University, Tegan moved to the Dallas/Fort Worth Area, where Tyler had also settled.

But our initial introduction to Tegan was briefly met with a touch of apprehension. Here was Tyler – a dashing blend of athleticism, talent, and focused – introducing us to a girlfriend who was equally athletic, talented, and purpose-driven. A committed relationship was a first for him. Tyler shared his life with friends during high school but never presented a girlfriend. This shift intrigued us. As parents, it is instinctual to be protective, and a sentiment echoed strongly by Alexia, who mirrored my sister Raschunda's protective streak when I introduced Bonita to her years ago.

As we met Tegan for the first time, it became apparent that she radiated a genuine and giving spirit. Any lingering reservations melted away by the end of that first dinner with Tegan in Iowa. It felt like Tyler had struck gold, having found someone so rare and valuable amidst the vastness of life's journey. Their commitment to each other was palpable, further underscored by their shared tales of selfless deeds.

One story, in particular, stands out. Tegan spoke of a stray cat wandering around Jack Trice Stadium. While most would have left it at that, she ensured it was fed and went the extra mile to give it a home. Today, that cat, Trice, is a testament to Tegan's kindness and is now an adored family member – in Dallas/Fort Worth.

Our numerous trips to Iowa were pivotal in forging our bond as a couple and deepening our connection to our children. When Tegan entered our lives, her unwavering devotion to Tyler was evident, gifting Alexia a future sister-in-law and blessing Bonita and me with a daughter-in-law we already hold close to our hearts. As life has come full circle, we now find ourselves extending that protective embrace to Tegan.

Rekindling the Marital Bond

In our first 23 years of marriage, Bonita and I realized the importance of not just focusing on raising our children but also nurturing our bond. We embarked on trips as a couple, recognizing the need for shared experiences to continue growing together.

We treasured the family vacations and the enriching experiences they provided, which helped shape our children into well-rounded individuals. However, we realized it was time for Bonita and me to create new experiences to continue to grow together versus apart. This is not to say that we no longer vacation with our children, but rather that we recognized the importance of nurturing our relationship as a couple.

Our decision was influenced by observing numerous examples of couples who supported their children wholeheartedly but ultimately divorced shortly after their children graduated high school or college. It became evident that their common bond revolved solely around their shared role as parents, leading them to believe there was no longer a need to remain together once their children reached adulthood. The empty nest syndrome struck its blow.

Consciously dedicating time to our relationship, Bonita and I aim to keep our connection robust as our children journey into independence. This intention stems from our reflections on challenges other couples face, which we have always been open about discussing.

The Pandemic – Bonita as a Beacon in the Darkness

As the pandemic darkened our world, Bonita's inherent brilliance within our family only intensified. My business trips subsided, but she took a bold step forward, taking on her pivotal role as a Respiratory Therapist with unwavering dedication.

This period brought about a renaissance for Respiratory Therapists. Historically overshadowed in healthcare, they suddenly became pivotal. Amidst the devastating spread of COVID-19, these unsung heroes, adept with specialized life-saving skills, found themselves at the forefront of medical care. Their expertise in operating intricate life-supporting machinery became invaluable. And while many therapists transitioned to on-the-road roles, tempted by significant salary hikes, Bonita's commitment to family and stability never wavered.

Our cherished family dinners, once filled with tales of my global adventures, transformed into heartfelt sessions. Each evening, we were captivated by Bonita's front-line accounts – the harrowing challenges, the mix of despair and hope, and the relentless battle against the virus. Beyond the stories, her personal growth and adaptability truly inspired us. She evolved, not just practicing her profession but exemplifying strength and empathy during trying times.

The broader world recognized and lauded her and her peers for their pivotal contributions. Yet, the intimate tokens of gratitude, closer to home, struck a chord. The hospital's commendations and heartfelt appreciation from patients and their families celebrated her professional expertise and compassionate care. The frequent accolades highlighting her comforting presence during a patient's dire moments were a testament to her character.

Amid the grueling shifts in the COVID unit and the emotional strain the pandemic brought, Bonita's unwavering commitment to her patients shone through in ways that extended beyond her medical expertise. One morning, en route to her 12-hour shift, she spotted a "Silver Alert" sign by the road, indicating a lost elderly individual whose disappearance had prompted a state-wide search. Days later, while caring for a John Doe in her unit – a man who had been tended to by numerous healthcare workers without anyone recognizing his potential connection to the Silver Alert – Bonita's instincts and empathetic nature guided her to a potential realization.

Could their John Doe be the very man the state was desperately trying to locate? With a heart driven by concern, she approached the hospital's management with her suspicions. After a series of verifications and calls, her hunch proved right: their unidentified patient was indeed the Silver Alert target, who had traveled a staggering 350 miles and was now far from home, disoriented, and unable to recall his own identity.

Bonita's keen observation and the initiative had done more than provide medical care; she set in motion a reunion, bringing solace to a distressed family. This incident showcased not only her medical acumen but also the depth of her commitment to her patients as individuals, her ability to see beyond the obvious, and her unwavering sense of humanity.

The transformation of Bonita into a dedicated Respiratory Therapist could easily have introduced a chasm between us. Such demanding roles often do, consuming time and emotional bandwidth, leaving couples grappling with the ever-widening distance. However, with Bonita, the opposite held true. Her unyielding commitment to her profession mirrored the very essence of our bond. The same giving spirit that propelled her to work tirelessly in the hospital was the very same force that kept the heart of our relationship beating strong.

Witnessing Bonita the R.T., I was not only seeing a dedicated healthcare worker but also the woman I fell in love with, whose enduring spirit always sought to give, both in her professional and personal life. The same love that had her soothing anxious patients and guiding lost souls back to their families was the love she brought home, ensuring that we never drifted apart. It was a testament to the fact that true dedication, whether to a cause or to a relationship, is not about the time spent but the quality of the moments shared.

In a world where many pursued fleeting gains, Bonita exemplified the essence of genuine commitment, always prioritizing the heart and soul of a matter over transient rewards. This inherent strength of character didn't just make her an outstanding R.T., but also an unwavering anchor in our shared life journey.

Relationships Under the Microscope: The Pandemic's Revealing Nature

During the height of the pandemic, we observed a transformative shift in the relationships around us. It wasn't just the virus that spread; a wave of introspection was equally pervasive. The pandemic, for many, acted as an uninvited litmus test for relationships, forcing couples to confront whether they had unwittingly drifted apart over the years.

Several couples spent unprecedented time together due to lockdowns and work-from-home mandates. This intensified togetherness acted as a double-edged sword. For some, it was an opportunity to reconnect, reminisce, and rekindle their bond. However, for many others, it was a glaring spotlight on issues simmering beneath the surface, often ignored in the hustle and bustle of pre-pandemic life.

Many discovered that they hadn't effectively communicated with their partners for a long time. Prior, with busy schedules, it was easier to sweep disagreements under the rug. But now, confined within four walls, unresolved arguments, and miscommunications became more pronounced, leading to increased tension. These tensions included the following:

- **Trust Issues:** The pandemic was a time of stress and uncertainty. For some, this brought to light betrayals and hidden secrets that eroded trust. Discovering infidelities or financial indiscretions during such a tense period left many couples feeling vulnerable and betrayed.

- **Financial Strains:** Many couples faced significant financial pressures from job losses and economic downturns. Those who hadn't previously discussed or aligned on money were at odds, often leading to blame games and resentments.

- **Different Coping Mechanisms:** Everyone has their way of dealing with stress and anxiety. The pandemic magnified these differences. While one partner might have sought solace in work, another might have felt the need for increased emotional connection. Misunderstandings arose when these needs clashed or were not communicated.

- **Lost Shared Interests:** Over time, some couples realized they had evolved differently, developing separate interests and hobbies. With its limited external distractions, the pandemic brought this divergence to the forefront, making some question their compatibility.

While many relationships navigated these challenges successfully by finding ways to grow together, others realized they had been growing apart far longer than they'd recognized. In its unforgiving nature, the pandemic acted as a mirror, reflecting the true state of many unions.

Rediscovering Togetherness

As life evolves, couples face the danger of growing apart rather than growing together. The shifting sands of individual pursuits, changing careers, and life's inevitable phases can create distances, sometimes unnoticed. What binds us during these times? The magic often lies in shared experiences.

These moments of togetherness – the highs and lows of raising kids, overcoming life's obstacles, or exploring new worlds together – forge bonds that stand the test of time. When kids grow up and venture out independently, couples stand at a pivotal crossroads. This empty nest phase could herald feelings of loneliness, but it also holds the potential for rediscovery.

Bonita and I took this time as an invitation to rekindle and reinforce our bond. As the world around us began to heal and reopen, we delved into shared adventures. Traveling to places new to both of us, like the scenic drives to Arkansas to visit our daughter or dancing away at concerts, these experiences weren't just trips; they were a reiteration of our commitment to each other. While family outings, especially with our kids, always held their own charm, our duo adventures unfolded as chapters of renewed intimacy.

Importantly, rediscovering togetherness doesn't always mean it's just the two of you against the world. Bonita and I find immense joy in the presence of our kids, relishing the comfort and familiarity when they're around. Every relationship is unique. While the end goal is a revitalized sense of unity, the journey can be tailored. Whether with kids, friends, or just the two of you, your chosen path should resonate with your shared values and aspirations.

Over time, I've realized that relationships, much like gardens, need tending to bloom. They demand time, effort, and a sprinkle of adventure now and then. Our journey, with its ups and downs and our conscious effort to weave in shared experiences, reinforces a simple truth: the essence of a strong bond isn't about sidestepping challenges but facing them side by side.

Strategies for Improvement

The journey of life brings with it evolution and change. Over time, partners may find their paths diverging, leading to feelings of detachment or lost intimacy. These aren't mere shifts in preferences or habits but deep-seated evolutions in beliefs, aspirations, and life perspectives. While individual growth is inevitable and desirable, it is crucial to ensure that this growth doesn't erode the shared foundation.

For couples facing this drift, the emphasis should be on reconnection, rediscovery, and rejuvenation. Embracing shared experiences, setting aside moments for mutual introspection, and understanding each other's evolving dreams and aspirations are all steps toward ensuring that while two people might change, their shared journey remains interwoven, celebrating individuality and unity.

Drawing from academic research, the strategies outlined in the subsequent sections offer guidance to couples aiming to keep their emotional bonds strong and their marriage resilient:

- **Prioritize Quality Time:** Committing to regular quality time can rekindle emotional intimacy. Uninterrupted moments foster deeper understanding and appreciation (Aron, Norman, Aron, & Lewandowski, 2002).

- **Revisit Shared Goals and Dreams:** Regularly revisiting and updating shared aspirations can rejuvenate the bond and sense of a shared journey (Litzinger & Gordon, 2005).

- **Practice Emotional Check-ins:** Systematic emotional check-ins help gauge the emotional pulse of the relationship, allowing early interventions if needed (Duncan, Coatsworth, & Greenberg, 2009).

- **Cultivate Shared Experiences:** Engaging in new activities or learning can bolster connection and create fresh memories (Reissman, Aron, & Bergen, 1993).

- **Seek Couples' Therapy:** Engaging in therapy can provide structured guidance and tools to bridge emotional distances (Gurman & Fraenkel, 2002).

- **Strengthen Attachment Security:** Emphasizing behaviors that enhance attachment security can combat feelings of emotional drift (Mikulincer, Shaver, & Pereg, 2003).

Reflective Prompts

Finally, here are three questions to ask yourself to prevent growing apart in your marriage:

1. **Shared Interests and Activities:** Reflect on the activities you and your partner once enjoyed together. Are there hobbies or pastimes that have been set aside over the years? How might reintroducing or discovering new shared interests bridge the emotional distance?

2. **Moments of Connection:** Think about the moments that sparked joy or intimacy in your relationship. How often do you experience these now? Consider ways to intentionally create opportunities for connection, whether through date nights, deep conversations, or spontaneous adventures.

3. **Personal Growth and Support:** Recognize that individual growth is a natural part of life. How can you support each other's personal journeys while ensuring the relationship remains a mutual priority?

_____

_____

_____

_____

_____

_____

CHAPTER 5

Lack of Intimacy and Emotional Connection

Reviving Intimacy, Deepening Connection

The soft glow from the TV lit the room, but its light couldn't bridge the growing divide between Stella and Rashad. Their evenings had become all too predictable: dinner, some TV, then off to bed. Conversations that once flowed with passion and depth now felt like mere exchanges of daily formalities.

Rashad shifted, taking a lingering glance at Stella. The physical space on the couch felt symptomatic of a deeper emotional void. It wasn't lost on either of them that their bond had changed, but the reasons remained unspoken.

Mustering courage, Rashad turned off the TV, embracing the profound silence that filled the room. "Stella," he ventured, voice laden with vulnerability, "do you ever feel... distant? Like we're right next to each other, but miles apart in our hearts?"

She met his gaze, eyes swimming with a mix of sorrow and understanding. "Every single day, Rashad. I feel it too. I miss us. The real us. I miss the days when our hearts would speak before our mouths did."

Rashad took a deep breath, their hands tentatively finding each other, "It's like we've become roommates who share memories. We used to dream together, laugh at the smallest things, and now... it feels like we're drifting."

Stella's voice quivered, "It scares me, Rashad. How did we get here? I want us to find our spark again. I need to feel that connection, that intimacy we once had."

Their conversation was raw and revealing, laying bare the realities of their emotional estrangement. But it was also a step, perhaps the first in a long time, towards understanding and reclaiming the closeness they once cherished. The journey ahead was uncertain, but the intent to bridge the divide was clear.

Setting the Stage

Intimacy and emotional connection, much like the deep roots of an ancient tree, anchor and nourish the relationship, providing stability during life's turbulent storms. These elements are not merely the physical closeness often associated with marital unions but encompass the profound emotional and spiritual bond that transforms a relationship from fleeting attraction to a deep, life-long commitment. When this bond weakens or is absent, the very essence of the relationship is at risk, casting shadows of doubt, loneliness, and despair.

At the inception of most relationships, couples often find themselves in the throes of passion and a seemingly unbreakable emotional connection. Every moment is charged with discovery, understanding, and mutual admiration. Yet, as time passes, the demands of daily life, external pressures, or unresolved conflicts can erode this intimacy. The once effervescent connection can wane, leaving partners isolated, even in the same room.

This chapter delves deep into the caverns of intimacy and emotional connection, shedding light on the factors that can inadvertently create emotional chasms between partners. We will explore the nuanced differences between emotional and physical intimacy, underscoring the importance of both in a flourishing marital landscape.

Through this journey, you will be equipped to recognize the silent symptoms of dwindling intimacy and be empowered with strategies to reignite the emotional flame. It is a call to action for every couple, urging them to prioritize the emotional mosaic of their union, ensuring that the threads of intimacy and connection remain vibrant, resilient, and ever-evolving.

Before proceeding, it's essential to explore the research related to this topic.

In-Depth Research Dive

Lack of intimacy and emotional connection, particularly in marital relationships, has been extensively studied in family psychology. According to Weiss (1975), losing intimate companionship, or the emotional void created by a partner's detachment, is a primary precursor to marital dissatisfaction. It is not only the absence of positive interactions, such as warmth and understanding that leads to discontent but also the onset of negative behaviors, such as criticism and blame.

This detachment has been associated with lower levels of relationship satisfaction and greater vulnerability to external marital threats.

Fincham, Beach, Harold, and Osborne (1997) explored the association between financial distress and marital quality in light of external stressors influencing emotional detachment. Their findings revealed that financial distress predicts negative marital interactions, with spousal conflict, decreased positive interactions, and a decline in perceived relationship stability being common outcomes. These negative marital interactions could further foster a lack of intimacy and emotional connection, highlighting the cascading effect external stressors might have on emotional intimacy.

Concerning the impact of mental health on marital intimacy, Whisman (2001) highlighted the implications of depression on marital satisfaction. Depressive symptoms in one or both partners were found to predict declines in marital satisfaction. Notably, the non-depressed partner also reported decreased relationship satisfaction, indicating the pervasive influence of mental health conditions on the relational ecosystem. Such findings illuminate the role of individual well-being in maintaining emotional closeness and highlight the mutual influence partners exert on each other's mental health.

The intricate relationship between emotional and physical intimacy was examined by Impett, Strachman, Finkel, and Gable (2008). They argued that while emotional intimacy leads to heightened physical intimacy, the inverse relationship is more nuanced. Periods of low emotional intimacy could lead to reductions in physical intimacy, but actively engaging in physical intimacy during such periods could serve as a pathway to reinstate emotional connection. Their findings underscore the reciprocity between emotional and physical intimacy and offer an avenue for couples to bridge emotional distances.

Building upon a lack of intimacy and emotional connection and its correlation to marital satisfaction, Doss, Simpson, and Christensen (2004) delved into the role of interventions in reversing this pattern. They noted that couples therapy, particularly Integrative Behavioral Couple Therapy (IBCT), positively impacted marital satisfaction and emotional connection. Through techniques that promote acceptance and change, partners were better equipped to handle emotional disconnects, reducing the risks of estrangement. Emphasizing that early intervention was critical, the study found that couples who sought therapy sooner rather than later were more likely to rebuild emotional intimacy and reduce detachment.

While interventions like therapy can be effective, understanding the origins of emotional detachment is equally critical. Sanders, Halford, and Behrens (1999) investigated the role of communication in marital satisfaction. Poor communication skills were identified as a significant factor leading to a lack of intimacy and emotional connection, with couples frequently reporting feeling unheard or misunderstood. By improving these skills, the study posits, couples can reduce misunderstandings, preemptively address potential conflicts, and foster a healthier emotional environment. Hence, effective communication is a cornerstone of marital well-being and emotional connectedness.

Delving into parenthood, Lawrence, Rothman, Cobb, Rothman, and Bradbury (2008) examined the transition to this new role and its impact on marital satisfaction. Their findings pointed toward a decline in marital satisfaction post-childbirth, largely attributed to reduced emotional intimacy. The demands and responsibilities of parenting and the diminished time for couple intimacy can foster a lack of intimacy and emotional connection. However, couples who maintained regular connection rituals, like date nights or open dialogues about their feelings, fared better in maintaining their emotional bonds.

Lastly, it is essential to understand the role of individual growth and its potential influence on emotional intimacy. According to Rusbult, Martz, and Agnew (1998), the investment model of relationships proposes that satisfaction is not only based on the rewards and costs currently experienced but also on the investments made in the relationship. As individuals grow and evolve, their prioritized investments might shift, potentially leading to a lack of intimacy and emotional connection if not communicated and understood. This highlights the importance of mutual growth and continuous reinvestment in the relationship to nurture emotional intimacy.

Reflections and Insights

Lack of Intimacy and Emotional Connection: From Virtual Boardrooms to Bedroom Talks

During an enlightening virtual session with one of my executive coaching clients – a conversation now common in our era of remote work – I observed a unique trend on her LinkedIn profile. Despite being in a world where personal branding on digital platforms speaks volumes, her profile seemed muted about her current company and her recognized role as an industry speaker. On probing, she unveiled a feeling of detachment, giving her complete potential to her role yet not marrying her extensive skills to the company's digital brand presence.

In today's age, where digital impressions often precede face-to-face interactions, intimacy in personal relationships isn't just about physical proximity but emotional resonance. Similarly, in a corporate setting, the lack of intimacy isn't just about being physically present in an office. With many working remotely, it's about feeling aligned and connected to a company's digital ethos and larger purpose.

I remember my transitional phase, navigating the challenges of connecting with a company's virtual culture. When I joined Microsoft in a world transitioning to the digital age, there was a self-reflection phase and a digital identity crisis. However, under the mentorship of an inspiring female director who saw the future of remote collaborations, I redefined my role, making it more virtually visible and globally connected. I didn't just execute tasks; I became an emblem of Microsoft's evolving digital identity.

This journey mirrors the nuances of intimacy in today's relationships. With digital interactions being a significant part of modern relationships, emotional connections extend beyond personal interactions to digital ones. Similarly, in the corporate realm, employees now have the dual task of aligning with a company's online and offline persona. In marriages, it's about ensuring connections are maintained, not just in shared spaces but in shared online experiences. A seamless integration of offline and online intimacy, bolstered by appreciation and mutual growth, becomes pivotal to thriving in both.

The Evolving Nature of Intimacy and Connection

Bonita and I, like many couples, started our journey under the enchanting belief that the fires of intimacy and emotional connection would forever burn bright. In those initial stages of romance, even a fleeting thought or a glance at our partner ignited profound passion. However, as years passed, we learned that while the flame never truly dies, it occasionally needs rekindling.

With time, several factors can subtly encroach upon those spontaneous moments of intimacy. Health issues might modify how we express physical closeness, while accumulated shared experiences can occasionally obscure our perception of our partners. Past events or dormant biases could sometimes deter us from being truly present. This highlights the pivotal realization that intimacy and connection demand consistent attention and nurturing. This becomes especially relevant when faced with challenges like the grief of loss, financial strains, or occasional misunderstandings tied to deciphering each other's love languages.

Our past discussions have shed light on the deliberate measures Bonita, and I have adopted to bolster our connection amidst life's ever-changing landscape. While our journey has been punctuated with challenges, the beacon of our shared love and commitment has perpetually guided us. I must often set aside my "Dr. Alford" persona and fully immerse myself as a devoted husband and father.

Concurrently, I've understood that for Bonita, her primary love language is physical touch. This means she deeply values and feels loved through physical gestures, from reassuring hugs to holding hands. These gestures aren't just signs of affection for her; they are affirmations of our bond, her individuality, and her dreams and feelings.

As we navigated these evolving facets of our relationship, an unexpected incident further illuminated the depth and nuances of intimacy for us. A seemingly random and unforeseen accident served as a stark reminder of how fragile life is. It forced us to confront and deeply reflect on what intimacy truly means in the face of adversity and life's unexpected turns. This incident wasn't just a physical ordeal but a profound emotional journey, pushing us to reevaluate and recommit to our bond in ways we hadn't previously fathomed.

From Despair to Catastrophe: A Flip That Changed Everything

Life's unpredictability became all too apparent roughly 15 years into our journey together. Reeling from the loss of my grandmother, I sank into deep melancholy, which Bonita keenly observed.

Seeing the healing potential in family gatherings, she urged me to attend my nephew's events. Gregory's college awards ceremony was a 50-mile journey, and Christian's birthday was a more distant trek. Though Bonita is fiercely independent, the idea of her traversing long country roads alone felt inadvisable, especially given my fragile state. We always faced challenges together, and this was no exception.

Christian's birthday took place at a gymnastics facility. The sight of the equipment rocketed me back to my Dallas youth, where we improvised sports due to a lack of formal facilities. Chatting with Greg, the birthday boy's father, I regaled him with tales of audacious backyard flips. The party's vibrant atmosphere and my nostalgia compelled me to attempt a flip, longing to recapture a fragment of my past.

The festive atmosphere took a harrowing turn when I landed with a broken neck. The previously lively gymnasium was silenced, except for my son's haunting cry. On the cold mat, unable to move, paralyzed from the neck down, Bonita's comforting words became my anchor amidst the growing dread. Her reassurances resonated even as the distant wail of an approaching ambulance grew louder.

At the hospital, every medical professional's face betrayed deep concern. The gravity of my injury – the paralysis, the risks – weighed heavily upon them. Yet, amidst this uncertainty, Bonita remained my constant lifeline, as her touch on my forehead was the only feeling part of my body.

I paradoxically prayed for more pain in the ICU's serene setting, viewing it as a beacon of life. Every waking moment, punctuated by the persistent beeps of machines, reminded me of the uphill battle ahead.

As days passed, I noted three constants: the unchanged numbness that imprisoned my body, the rotation of medical professionals whose faces oscillated between hope and concern, and Bonita, whose steadfast commitment never waned.

The Profound Depth of Intimacy: Beyond Just the Physical

Lying there, immobilized, my mind raced. The thought haunted me: what if this condition became permanent? I tried to recall the last intimate moment with Bonita, the gravity of the idea hitting me – it might have been our last. Yet, as I was enveloped in Bonita's unwavering gaze, filled with such palpable love and concern, I felt more profound intimacy than we had ever shared. This was not about touch or physical closeness but a deeper connection, revealing our bond's true essence.

At that vulnerable juncture, I recognized our love was not just skin deep. It soared beyond the confines of my damaged physique, flourishing in the unspoken emotional ties we had nurtured over the years. Bonita was a testament to the fact that the strength of our bond was not rooted solely in physical intimacy. Instead, it stemmed from shared memories, trials, victories, and the unwavering support we continually offered one another. With my future uncertain, doubts swirled. Would I ever feel again as I once did? Could we ever regain the physical closeness we took for granted?

But as I lay there, vulnerable and questioning, I began to understand the profound value of the simple, everyday moments we had shared. The gentle cuddles, the heartfelt kisses, and the comforting embraces held a depth of meaning that I had overlooked before. These seemingly ordinary gestures became symbols of our enduring love and reminded me of their profound significance in our relationship.

From Despair to Recovery

During those initial days, I was confined to quadriplegia, completely dependent on others for my basic needs. Every day was a battle as I embarked on the arduous journey of learning to walk, touch, move, and work again.

It was a daunting process, but today, I stand in awe of the new life and testimony God has granted me to have a longer life with Bonita and my kids. It is a testament that no one can truly comprehend how close I came to death or lifelong paralysis.

In the year following my life-altering accident, Bonita and I found ourselves on an uncharted path of transformation. Bonita had nurtured me through the tumultuous seas of recovery. She breathed life into our vows of "for better or worse," making me realize the true depth of those words. I had never experienced such profound dependence on another before; it was a humbling testament to our shared human fragility.

With my sister Raschunda serving in the U.S. Army and my mother Clara and grandmother Lillie Mae now in heaven, Bonita shouldered a role well beyond what I dreamed of as a committed wife. She became my anchor in a time of profound upheaval. As the rhythm of life marked the passing of days into weeks and weeks into months, we charted our course through this new reality together. Our journey was discovering and embracing fresh channels of love and intimacy amidst adversity.

During this period, progress was gradual yet consistent. My accident occurred 100 miles from home, and so did the surgery and my initial recovery. Fortunately, the surgery was successful. While my motor function remained limited, the doctors emphasized that much of my recovery would now depend on my determination.

I was soon given the green light to be transferred to a rehabilitation facility closer to home. It was only five miles from our house. This was a welcome development. It not only allowed Bonita some semblance of normalcy, given that she had been unwaveringly by my side, but it also brought me nearer to my son, who had returned to school. Meanwhile, my daughter, studying in a college over 600 miles away, remained somewhat shielded from the extent of our ordeal as we tried our best to keep her from undue worry.

A Night of Resilience

One night in the rehabilitation hospital remains etched vividly in my memory. Struggling with the pain from my atrophied muscles, I found comfort in Bonita's presence. She held my hand in the dimly lit room, her eyes brimming with compassion and strength. "We are in this together, baby," she whispered, her words of resolve echoing in the room's silence. They became my mantra during the grueling days of physical therapy.

This experience opened doors to newfound levels of honesty and openness between us. Our conversations delved deeper, unearthing fears, dreams, and thoughts previously unshared. We forged a connection transcending physical barriers, creating transformative emotional and spiritual intimacy.

Yet, this journey extended beyond physical recovery and mutual support. It was a path to my personal growth and transformation. My misgivings were not rooted in Bonita's understanding of love or dedication but in my misconceptions.

Growing up, I harbored skewed perceptions of love and loyalty. However, witnessing Bonita's unwavering support during my trials clarified my misguided belief: "If you give 100%, you will be hurt 100%." Her steadfast devotion broke down the barriers I had erected around my heart.

For all our years together, while Bonita remained steadfast in her trust and love, I held back, hesitant to fully embrace the vulnerability that comes with total trust. Even when faced with our toughest trials, she chose to stand firmly by my side, offering boundless support and love. This act underscored that my real challenge wasn't with Bonita but with my ingrained fears and misconceptions.

It was a painful realization that I needed the traumatic experience of breaking my neck to understand this truly. This ordeal aided my physical recovery and reshaped my perspective on trust, commitment, and the essence of emotional vulnerability.

Cherishing Every Moment: Beyond Physical Intimacy

Life comprises many moments, some seemingly trivial and others profoundly life-changing. The key to a deep, lasting relationship is recognizing the intrinsic value in every shared moment. In these interactions, however fleeting, lies the opportunity to fortify the bonds of intimacy and understand its multifaceted nature.

Yet, how often do we stop and genuinely contemplate the foundation of our connection with our partner? If, hypothetically, the gift of physical intimacy was suddenly stripped away, would the relationship still stand resilient? Or would it crumble, revealing a fragile bond that was overly reliant on just one facet of intimacy?

During my paralysis, this hypothetical scenario became a daunting reality for Bonita and me. Faced with the potential loss of physical closeness, we were thrust into uncharted territory. We grappled with the challenging question: If physical touch, a language we had always known, was no longer a part of our lexicon, could our love still communicate? Could it still thrive?

Our society has constructed certain notions around relationships and masculinity. The prevalent belief is that a man's worth and ability to be a partner are deeply intertwined with his physical capabilities. For far too long, masculinity has been defined by physical strength and dominance. In such a construct, physical intimacy becomes a validation of a man's role in a relationship, an affirmation of his masculinity.

But isn't this a narrow lens through which to view intimacy? Intimacy, in its truest form, is so much more than physical. It is about shared dreams and mutual aspirations. It's about those late-night vulnerable conversations when every mask falls off. It's about navigating life's challenges together with shared purpose and understanding.

For Bonita and me, our forced separation from physical intimacy illuminated the depth and richness of our emotional and spiritual connection. We discovered layers to our relationship that might have remained obscured otherwise. The inability to express love through touch drove us to seek other avenues, and in doing so, we stumbled upon pockets of intimacy we hadn't known existed.

It's a challenging notion to confront, especially for men conditioned by societal expectations. But imagine a world where every man recognizes that his true strength doesn't lie just in his physical prowess but in his ability to connect, empathize, and truly understand his partner. Imagine relationships where couples continuously explore and celebrate every facet of intimacy, not just the physical.

In essence, our shared ordeal acted as a crucible, testing the strength of our relationship. And from it emerged a refined understanding of what it means to be truly connected. It became clear that a bond built on shared experiences, mutual respect, emotional support, and spiritual alignment is unbreakable and deeply fulfilling.

Recovering from paralysis provided an unparalleled lesson on the value of second chances. When I regained my ability to be physically intimate, each moment of closeness bore an entirely new significance. A simple embrace was no longer just an act of affection; it was a symbol of triumph over adversity, a reminder of the fragility of life, and an expression of gratitude. The layers of intimacy that Bonita and I had unearthed during our challenging period amplified the depth of our physical connection. The correlation became evident: the more layers of intimacy a relationship harbors, the closer partners tend to feel toward each other.

Ten years have passed since the accident, and with the wisdom of hindsight, I've come to appreciate how life's experiences continuously reshape our perspectives. Our understanding of intimacy, like all things, is not static. It evolves, morphs, and adapts based on our experiences, trials, and learnings. As individuals, our views on intimacy can shift over time, influenced by personal growth and experiences.

This evolution is natural and even essential for personal gain. However, what becomes crucial in a relationship is ensuring that as our individual views on intimacy evolve, they remain aligned with our partner's.

Open communication plays a pivotal role here. It's essential to regularly take stock of our feelings, to discuss them openly with our partners, and to ensure we are both on the same page. Just as a tree needs constant nurturing to bear fruit, a relationship requires continuous effort to ensure the bond remains strong, vibrant, and aligned.

So, for every couple navigating the journey of love, cherish every shared moment, dream, and challenge. Let them be reminders that intimacy is a vast, beautiful tapestry woven with threads far more varied and profound than the physical alone. Challenge yourselves to explore its depths, for in doing so, you might discover treasures that redefine your understanding of love and connection.

Strategies for Improvement

The ties that bind a couple go beyond shared experiences and memories. At the heart of every thriving marriage lies intimacy, a profound emotional and physical connection that nurtures and sustains the relationship. The absence of this closeness can lead to feelings of isolation, rendering partners like roommates rather than soulmates. Yet, intimacy isn't static; it's a continually evolving bond that requires nurturing.

For couples navigating this challenge, it's essential to remember that rekindling intimacy often begins with small, deliberate actions: honest conversations, meaningful gestures, and creating spaces for vulnerability. By prioritizing closeness and re-establishing the channels of emotional expression, couples can rebuild the deep connection that once drew them together, ensuring their bond remains unbreakable.

The following strategies have been identified as paramount in maintaining marital intimacy and emotional connectedness:

- **Prioritize Physical Connection:** Regular physical touch, such as holding hands and hugging, has been found to release oxytocin, enhancing feelings of trust and bonding between partners (Field, 2010).

- **Engage in Shared Activities:** Pursuing mutual hobbies or interests strengthens the bond by creating shared memories and experiences (Reissman, Aron, & Bergen, 1993).

- **Establish Emotional Check-ins:** A routine of discussing feelings and emotional states helps recognize and address issues before they escalate (Bodenmann, Bradbury, & Pihet, 2009).

- **Practice Vulnerability:** Opening up about personal fears, hopes, and dreams fosters a deeper emotional connection (Neff & Karney, 2017).

- **Prioritize Quality Time:** Intentional, uninterrupted time allows couples to reconnect and reinforce their bond (Gable, Reis, Impett, & Asher, 2004).

- **Seek Professional Support:** Engaging in couples therapy can provide tools and strategies to navigate challenges and strengthen the emotional bond (Bradford, Burningham, Sandberg, & Johnson, 2017).

Reflective Prompts

Finally, here are three questions to ask yourself to deal with the lack of emotional connection in your marriage:

1. **Physical Touch and Closeness:** Ponder the moments when you feel most connected to your partner physically. Are there gestures, such as holding hands or hugging, that you've moved away from? Rediscover the power of touch in conveying love and affection.

2. **Emotional Vulnerability:** Reflect on the depth of your emotional exchanges. How open and vulnerable are you with your partner about your feelings, fears, and dreams? Consider creating safe spaces for these discussions to reignite emotional intimacy.

3. **Quality Time:** How often do you prioritize spending undistracted, quality time with your partner? Exploring ways to reconnect regularly, without the interruptions of daily life, can rekindle intimacy.

_____

_____

_____

_____

_____

_____

CHAPTER 6

Different Values and Goals

Aligning Values, Charting Together

The aroma of freshly brewed coffee filled the morning air as Grayson set the breakfast table. He glanced at the corner of their cozy living room where a packed suitcase stood, a testament to Shanique's upcoming mission trip to Africa.

Shanique entered the kitchen; her enthusiasm was palpable. "I can't believe I'll be helping build schools in Haiti! It has been a dream for so long."

Grayson nodded, trying to mask his frustration. "I understand, Shanique. But we also talked about saving for our dream home next year. A dream we share, right?"

Shanique's face fell, the conflict of their different aspirations evident. "Grayson, helping others, making a difference... it is important to me."

"And starting a family, having a stable home, that's important to me. Maybe we should just..." Grayson retorted, his voice edged with resentment. He trailed off, and Shanique did not hear the words, "Maybe we should just..."

They sat in silence, the chasm of their differing values and goals widening. The breakfast, once a daily ritual of love and sharing, had become a battleground of unmet expectations.

Shanique finally broke the silence. "We need to find a balance, Grayson. Your dreams matter to me, but I can't ignore mine."

Grayson sighed, realizing the truth in her words. "I love you, Shanique. We need to work together, even if our paths sometimes diverge. But at some point, we must agree on priorities, and having kids with you is at the top of my list."

Their journey was not about giving up individual dreams but finding a harmonious way to merge their paths, respecting and supporting each other's aspirations.

Setting the Stage

Values and goals are the compass and map of our life's journey. They guide our decisions, shape our aspirations, and influence our perceptions of success and fulfillment. In relationships, especially marital unions, these values and goals play a pivotal role in directing the course of the partnership. When two individuals come together, they bring with them not just their personal histories but also their beliefs, priorities, and visions for the future. When these align, they form a powerful synergy, propelling the relationship forward with shared purpose and understanding. Conversely, when they diverge, the journey becomes fraught with challenges, disagreements, and dissonance.

At the dawn of romance, love often acts as a unifying force, glossing over differences and painting a rosy picture of compatibility. Yet, as the initial euphoria settles and couples delve into the depths of building a life together, discrepancies in values and goals become more apparent. These might manifest as disagreements on financial priorities, divergent career aspirations, differing views on family planning, or even contrasting beliefs about the world.

This chapter will navigate the intricate landscape of values and goals within marital contexts. We will unearth the importance of recognizing, respecting, and reconciling differences, understanding that it is not always about convergence but often about coexistence.

The journey ahead will offer insights into the significance of open dialogue, mutual respect, and the art of compromise. It is a reminder that while love may be the cornerstone of a relationship, aligning values and goals solidifies its foundation, ensuring longevity, understanding, and mutual growth.

To begin, we should consider the studies conducted on this subject.

In-Depth Research Dive

Contrasting values and goals are at the heart of many marital disagreements. According to Stanley, Markman, and Whitton (2002), premarital education that seeks to uncover potential value disparities is pivotal in reducing subsequent marital distress and enhancing relationship satisfaction. Their research highlighted that couples who partook in premarital education had a more realistic understanding of expectations and were better equipped to handle discrepancies in values and goals. This fortified their bonds and reduced the divorce rate over the initial years of marriage.

Values related to finances are a recurring point of contention for many couples. According to Dew, Britt, and Huston (2012), financial disagreements are stronger predictors of divorce relative to other conflict topics. Couples with disparate monetary values and goals, such as differing views on saving, spending, or investing, reported more frequent and intense conflicts. The study underscores the importance of addressing financial values explicitly, as they intersect with broader life goals and day-to-day marital functioning.

The topic of children – whether or not to have them and how to raise them – is another area where contrasting values can emerge. Knoester and Eggebeen (2006) established that discrepancies in parental values and child-rearing goals can lead to decreased marital satisfaction. Differences in priorities related to child-rearing, disciplinary strategies, and educational aspirations for children can exacerbate marital stress. Over time, unresolved issues related to parenting can erode the relationship, highlighting the need for proactive alignment in parenting philosophies.

Religious and spiritual values, while foundational for many individuals, can also be sources of discord within marriages. According to Mahoney et al. (1999), spiritual discrepancies between partners – regarding beliefs, practices, and the role of faith in decision-making – were associated with increased marital conflict and reduced relationship satisfaction. Their research revealed that couples who lacked alignment in their spiritual beliefs or practices found it challenging to find mutual ground on significant life decisions, further emphasizing the importance of congruence in core values within marital relationships.

While many couples recognize the importance of communication in resolving differences, the role of communication in navigating contrasting values cannot be understated. According to Gottman and Levenson (2000), how couples communicate about their differences seems to have a greater impact on marital satisfaction and longevity than the existence of the differences themselves. Their research emphasized that couples who approached disagreements with mutual respect, understanding, and open-mindedness had more resilient and fulfilling marriages than those who relied on criticism, contempt, and defensiveness.

Cultural and background differences, encompassing traditions, beliefs, and familial practices, present another layer of contrasting values. Citing the work of Helms, Supple, and Proulx (2011), marriages in which partners hail from different cultural backgrounds might experience pronounced challenges due to variances in family expectations, traditions, and values. The study found that cross-cultural couples who proactively acknowledged, respected, and integrated aspects of both cultures into their shared life reported higher levels of marital satisfaction. Recognizing cultural values and addressing them collaboratively fostered mutual understanding and respect.

Likewise, the dynamic nature of values and goals necessitates continuous alignment and reevaluation in marital relationships. A longitudinal study by Huston, Niehuis, and Smith (2001) found that couples' values and goals naturally evolve, influenced by life experiences, personal growth, and external circumstances. Their research highlighted that marital satisfaction was associated with the initial alignment of values and how couples navigated shifts in priorities and aspirations throughout the marriage journey. It underscores the importance of ongoing dialogue and mutual adaptation as life changes.

Another intriguing dimension to consider is the role of social networks in shaping and reinforcing marital values. Julien, Markman, and Lindahl (1989) revealed that the support and beliefs of friends and family play a substantial role in the stability and satisfaction of marriages. When external social networks affirm and support a couple's values and goals, couples experience validation and increased cohesion. Conversely, if the couple's values diverged significantly from their social network's norms, they often faced external pressure and potential strain on their relationship.

Reflections and Insights

Different Values and Goals: From Boardroom to Bedroom

Every organization boasts a distinct culture defined by shared values, norms, and beliefs that drive its operations. Similarly, when two individuals form a union in marriage, they create their unique relational culture, drawing from their backgrounds, traditions, and values. The parallels between entering an organization and entering a marriage are strikingly similar in their foundational stages.

Today's corporate landscape underscores the importance of alignment. New hires aren't just evaluated based on their technical abilities. The interview loops, psychometric assessments, and problem-solving evaluations aim to discern if the potential employee can assimilate and enhance the company's culture. In the digital age, potential employees empowered by technology can delve deep into a company's ethos. They peruse social media, review sites, and annual reports to discern if the company's values align with theirs. This due diligence parallels the investigative phase of courtship in relationships, where each partner gauges alignment with the other's values, aspirations, and life outlooks.

Yet, the intersection between business recruitment and marital union runs deeper than the initial evaluative stage. Just as a company's culture is driven by its core values, an individual's behavior in a relationship is largely governed by personal beliefs and values. In businesses, misalignment can lead to decreased productivity or even employee turnover. In marriages, dissonance in core values can manifest as frequent conflicts, dissatisfaction, or separation.

Businesses are evolving rapidly in the era of start-up cultures, remote work, and flexible roles. A company's values aren't just about profit; they encompass work-life balance, social responsibility, diversity, and inclusion. Similarly, contemporary marriages are not just about traditional roles or staying together. They involve navigating dual careers, blended families, and evolving gender roles. Just as businesses have to revisit their values to remain relevant, couples must communicate and recalibrate their shared goals amidst life's changes.

Embracing Unity amidst Differences: The Dance of Shared and Unique Values in Marriage

Every relationship is woven with threads of shared values, individual beliefs, and unique quirks. As couples come together, they inevitably discover differences in their perspectives, experiences, and values. However, amidst these variations lies the magic formula for a thriving marriage. In my perspective, when we fall in love, we resonate deeply with about 80% of our partner's essence, while the remaining 20% might be areas of challenge or even disagreement. This 80-20 principle is not a fixed rule, but it offers an insightful lens through which we can view marital dynamics.

The core of a successful marriage revolves around ensuring that this predominant 80% aligns with the values you deem non-negotiable. Bonita and I have several shared values that are important to the health of our marriage such as Flexibility, Open communication, Respect, Empathy, Vulnerability, Empowerment, Resilience, Wellness, Emotional Intelligence, and Devotion. However, over the years, we simplified these to some cornerstone values such as honesty, prioritizing our children, setting a financial foundation, and maintaining a respectful and open mode of communication with each other and the world at large. This strong alignment created a sturdy foundation upon which our love and understanding flourished.

As for the remaining 20% – the quirks, the disagreements, the little things that sometimes irk us about our partners – it's essential to approach them with patience, understanding, and sometimes a sprinkle of humor. These are not necessarily deal-breakers but areas where growth, adaptation, and compromise come into play. I will not delve into our respective 20% specifics, and there's a significant reason. A major part of building trust in a relationship is ensuring that very few outside of the marriage are privy to your spouse's weaknesses.

Overemphasizing your partner's strengths and refraining from deconstructing them in public view is crucial. As your partner works on their weaknesses, those you've let in on those imperfections might judge them not by their growth but by what you once said. A core value I deeply uphold concerning Bonita is to never speak of her in a negative light. And thankfully, she remains discreet and does not broadcast to the world areas where I might not be as astute as many perceive. We've navigated our differences through mutual understanding and respect, strengthening our bond.

Setting the Foundation: Financial Values in Marriage

Marriage is often envisioned as a romantic union, but the merging of two distinct financial histories and philosophies lies beneath that. Before Bonita and I embarked on our shared journey, we delved deeply into our financial values and beliefs. The adage, "You only know what you know," rings particularly true in this realm. Through stories of past financial challenges and hopes for our children's well-roundedness and growth, we recognized the imperative of aligning our hearts and financial compasses.

Upon entering our union, I opened up about my financial history, including episodes I wasn't particularly proud of, like the theft case that miraculously didn't scar my permanent record. However, these weren't tales of regret but lessons in resilience.

On the flip side, while Bonita could turn to her father for aid in times of financial crisis, I carried with me a staunch principle: our financial trials and triumphs were ours alone. It was non-negotiable for me that my wife should ever feel the need to seek external financial support. If we faced adversity, it would be a testament to our commitment to grapple with and surmount it together.

This ethos was not born out of mere pride but a deep-seated belief that financial challenges, often touted as the leading disruptor in marriages, can also be a crucible for strengthening marital bonds. It's a test of trust, understanding, and mutual goal-setting. While many couples find themselves at loggerheads over financial disagreements, the willingness to understand, communicate, and align financial goals becomes a bedrock for a stable relationship.

Thus, as Bonita and I navigated the complexities of married life, our focus was not just on financial growth but on ensuring that our monetary values and goals were in sync. Financial stability isn't merely about wealth accumulation; it's about laying a resilient foundation for present challenges and future aspirations. It's about ensuring that both partners, regardless of their financial past, are on the same page, working together toward a shared future. This, I believe, is the cornerstone of a successful marital partnership.

Growing Together: Nurturing Shared Values

The evolution of our marriage was not just limited to finances; it was about aligning our personal values and weaving them into the fabric of our family life. We drew closer in our beliefs and aspirations with every chapter we added to our shared story. The trials we faced, the joyous moments we celebrated, and the lessons we learned along the way were not just personal experiences – they became the compass guiding our family.

Our belief in God and commitment to always seeking to do what is right shaped our decisions as a couple and as parents. While our faith was personal, we never aimed to push our beliefs onto others. Instead, we hoped to lead by example, showing our children the importance of kindness, empathy, and generosity. We realized that the legacy we wished to leave behind was not just about material inheritance but the values we upheld and the lessons we imparted.

For example, we embarked on a meaningful adventure together rather than buying our daughter a new car. We set aside a weekend to search for a budget-friendly cash car. Our efforts led us to Polly, a reliable and cherished vehicle that became a part of our family.

As time passed, Polly found a new purpose as we passed it down to my son, who affectionately renamed it Paul.

Eventually, we decided to pass on the legacy of Polly (Paul) to my nephew, hoping it would continue to serve him as faithfully as it had for us. Unfortunately, nature had different plans, and the car's journey ended abruptly when it faced the destructive force of a hailstorm.

At the heart of our family values was deliberately deprioritizing the question, "How much do you make?" Instead, we centered our decisions on a more profound inquiry, "What does buying them a new car as a teenager teach them? What do they have to look forward to when they achieve something beyond high school?"

These questions were significant and shaped our choices in guiding Alexia and Tyler. We wanted them to understand the value of hard work, perseverance, and the sense of accomplishment that comes from earning something through their efforts.

It is essential to note that our perspective is not a criticism of parents who choose to buy new cars for their children. By all means, if it aligns with a family's values and they are accustomed to the luxury of new vehicles, they should pass down those experiences to their children. After all, there isn't a one-size-fits-all blueprint for shared family values. Everyone's story is different, and every family's legacy is unique. Based on our life experiences and values, our narrative did not align with buying our children new cars at a young age.

Of course, life is full of unpredictable moments, and our conversations were not always smooth and flawless.

School Choices: Embracing Humility and Diversity

As the years unfolded, we encountered a pivotal moment: choosing our children's educational path. It is a decision that, for many, may seem straightforward, rooted in considerations of academic prestige or resource availability. But for us, it was deeply interwoven with our core values.

We cherished the memories and character-building lessons from our public school experiences. When faced with the societal pressure of enrolling our kids in private institutions, our compass pointed us toward a path less trodden. We decided to send our kids to a less privileged high school where they would gain more than just academic knowledge. We envisioned Alexia and Tyler learning invaluable lessons of compassion, humility and embracing diverse perspectives. It was not just about their capacity for understanding but also about the knowledge they would gain about the world and themselves.

Bonita and I knew the neighborhood school boasted greater resources, better extracurricular activities, and over-the-top events. However, we held a distinct vision for our children's education. Our desire was for them to experience the invaluable lessons of resilience and empathy, which we believed could be best learned at a school where not every student had the luxury of owning a car, after-school activities were not a given, and achievements were solely based on individual merit, unaffected by parental income.

This decision was not without its internal conflicts. Bonita and I grappled with the ramifications of our choice. Would sending our children to a less privileged school reflect our insecurities rooted in our past struggles, or would it be a genuine opportunity for them to develop shared values and a deep understanding of life's challenges? We pondered if this choice meant asking them to walk in our shoes when we did not have much or if it was genuinely about wanting them to foster empathy and resilience.

After much reflection, we both wholeheartedly agreed on the latter. We aspired for our children to understand the struggle and develop compassion for the less fortunate. We wanted them to recognize the spectrum of human experiences, valuing both the highs and the lows and grow into individuals who thrived in comfort and navigated challenges with grace and understanding.

Throughout our journey, there were moments when we needed to gently remind our children that their school experience might differ from their peers in the neighborhood.

One such instance was during my daughter Alexia's Sweet 16 party. Alexia asked that Bonita and I arrange transportation for her friends, who were on her basketball, track, or volleyball teams, understanding that not all parents prioritized supporting their children beyond sports. We rounded up several family members to pick up and drop off her classmates. We wanted our daughter to feel cherished and included in her special celebration, regardless of financial differences.

Similarly, there were times when my son Tyler expressed his desire to go to an amusement park with his bandmates, teammates, and friends. But Tyler's heart always shone brighter than his desires. On more than one occasion, he would approach us seeking a little extra stipend, not for himself, but to cover the costs for a friend who could not afford such an outing. This gesture, combined with similar acts of kindness from our daughter, was a clear indication that the legacy of giving, which Bonita and I had worked so diligently to instill, was taking root in their hearts.

Understanding that not everyone had the means for such leisurely activities, we always tried to guide our children toward a path of empathy and inclusivity. It was about fulfilling their wishes and teaching them the value of shared experiences, regardless of financial differences. The pride we felt in these moments was immeasurable, watching our children live and exemplify the values we held dear.

Living the Values: Generosity and Giving

Our values extended beyond our immediate family unit and into the broader community. As our children flourished, Bonita and I felt a profound call to give back, develop our blessings, and foster a supportive environment for all children. We did not seek recognition or accolades; our giving was driven by a heartfelt desire to make a difference.

Time and resources were generously donated to the schools our children attended, hoping to create a ripple effect of change and positivity. But our journey's beauty was witnessing our children absorbing these values. They observed and participated, understanding the transformative power of kindness and the lasting impact of genuine generosity. Whether in the story of our family car, Polly (later renamed Paul) or in the lessons taught through empathetic experiences, the spirit of giving was more than just an act – it became a way of life.

Though our actions were driven by sincere intent and not for acknowledgment, the universe has a way of reflecting the good one puts into the world. The community took note of our contributions, and while it was not our primary goal, recognition came in beautiful and unexpected ways. Bonita was honored with the esteemed

Lifetime PTA Member Award for her unwavering dedication. Similarly, the scholarship named after me at our children's high school was touching and humbling.

But beyond these accolades, the true reward lay in the knowledge that we were making a tangible difference. Every nod of appreciation, every silent acknowledgment, served as a testament to the deep-seated values we held dear. It reminded us that authentic acts of kindness and commitment ripple outward, touching lives in ways one might never fully grasp.

Legacy in Action: Our Children's Path

As stated earlier, one of the most profound affirmations of our values was witnessing their manifestation in our children. Alexia's journey was particularly heartwarming. She showed great promise in her high school's Law Magnet, which required acceptance and offered a curriculum similar to pre-law for those aspiring to attend law school. It would have been a natural choice, especially given her academic excellence. However, a pivotal moment in her education came during her final year. Her law teacher, Ms. Kaye, was battling cancer, yet her dedication to teaching and her students never wavered.

Ms. Kaye's resilience and her challenge to her students to make a genuine difference left a deep impression on Alexia. Inspired by Ms. Kaye's enduring spirit and plea to bring positive change, Alexia pivoted from a potential career in law. Instead, she chose a path in sociology and criminology, aspiring to delve deeper into societal structures and make impactful contributions as a professor. She graduated from Iowa State University with not one but three degrees, culminating in a Ph.D. in Sociology.

Tyler, in contrast, showcased a different method of giving back, demonstrating that there's more than one way to be altruistic. His financial habits were a puzzle initially. The money would come into his hands but seldom was spent on himself. Only after careful observation did we recognize his pattern: Tyler held onto his funds until someone in his circle was in dire need.

As he neared his college years, his ambition became clear. Tyler aspired to delve into the business world with a noble purpose. He was not aiming to amass wealth for personal gain. His vision was to earn great wealth to share with those in need generously. In his eyes, a business degree was a means to facilitate greater giving. He graduated from Iowa State University with not one but three business degrees – Marketing, Entrepreneurship, and Management.

Marriage: Navigating Differences in Values and Goals

Every marriage is a dance harmonizing two distinct values, dreams, and goals. Our union has been in shared aspirations and mutual respect, even in the face of differences. There were moments when our perspectives seemed to diverge, like when external influences painted pictures of material success. But instead of letting these differences create a chasm, we used them as opportunities for introspection, discussion, and growth.

It is natural for partners to have varied inclinations. Some might be drawn toward the allure of social prestige, while others find contentment in simplicity. But the real strength of a relationship lies in its ability to weather these differences, to find a middle ground, and to always come back to the shared core values that form the marriage's bedrock. Through understanding, patience, and communication, we have learned that our shared journey is richer because of the differences, not despite them.

Differences in values can manifest in the subtlest ways – a disagreement on spending habits, diverging opinions on child-rearing, or clashing views on societal issues – and these differences can magnify over time, creating deep chasms between partners. Such disparities go beyond mere lifestyle choices; they touch upon the essence of everyone, revealing contrasting views on purpose, meaning, and life's greater goals. When left unaddressed, these rifts can erode the trust and intimacy crucial for a marriage to thrive, leading to isolation and disillusionment. In such scenarios, the union is not just about two people coexisting; it becomes a tug-of-war of principles, with both parties feeling unheard and undervalued.

Having shared values in a marriage is not just a lofty ideal but a foundational pillar that ensures stability, mutual understanding, and harmony within the union. When two individuals come together to build a life, their values act as the compass, guiding decisions, influencing behaviors, and shaping their collective worldview. These deeply ingrained beliefs determine the priorities set within the household, the choices made for their family, and even how they communicate with one another. Without this shared compass, couples might find themselves lost in a sea of disagreements, feeling adrift and disconnected from each other's realities.

Faith and Understanding: Our Spiritual Compass

Given the rapid evolution of spiritual beliefs in today's world, it's acknowledged that many people lean into the concept of a higher power without necessarily adhering to organized religion. This is a testament to faith's fluidity and the universality of certain core values that transcend religious labels. One universally accepted principle, seen across cultures and belief systems, is the Golden Rule: Treating others as you wish to be treated.

Interestingly, the real test of this principle is not within the four walls of our homes, where love and familiarity often guide our actions. It emerges in the face of everyday challenges: How do we react in traffic when someone cuts us off? How do we handle situations where our food order is wrong or when service at a restaurant is slower than expected? How do we cope when professional ambitions don't pan out as we hoped, especially when we see peers advancing? Though seemingly mundane, these everyday moments truly test and reveal the depth of our values and beliefs.

For Bonita and me, our belief in God goes beyond a spiritual safety net or a Sunday ritual. Its compass consistently directs how we treat and interact with others. This faith is not merely about submitting to a higher authority but also about recognizing the divine in everyone we encounter. It prompts us to act patiently, understanding, and kindly, even when faced with challenges. It is a constant reminder that our interactions, big or small, reflect our values and, more significantly, our spiritual commitments.

While we never aimed to impose our beliefs on others, this spiritual foundation has undoubtedly influenced our values.

Strategies for Improvement

Everyone carries a compass of values and aspirations, guiding their life choices and shaping their identity. When two such compasses seem to point in different directions in a marriage, it can create turbulence. Disagreements stemming from contrasting beliefs or ambitions can be among the most challenging, as they touch upon the core of individual identities. However, such differences don't denote incompatibility. Instead, they represent an opportunity for enriched mutual understanding and growth. Couples can navigate these differences by seeking common ground, celebrating the shared aspects of their vision, and approaching differences with respect and curiosity. By doing so, they can craft a shared narrative that honors individual dreams and collective aspirations.

It is not uncommon for couples to discover unexpected deviations in their shared path, resulting in feelings of incompatibility. Proactive communication and understanding can assist couples in weaving their paths together, ensuring a harmonized journey through life's twists and turns.

Drawing from academic literature, here are several strategies to counteract the drift of different values and goals:

- **Revisit Shared Goals:** Periodically, ensure both partners align on shared long-term objectives and dreams, reinforcing the marital bond (Amato & Rogers, 1997).

- **Engage in Shared Activities:** Mutual hobbies or projects can cultivate shared experiences and memories, enhancing connection (Reissman, Aron, & Bergen, 1993).

- **Discuss Value Evolution:** Acknowledge and discuss how individual values may evolve and find common ground (Lauer, Lauer, & Kerr, 1990).

- **Foster Mutual Respect:** Understand and respect differing perspectives or life goals, even if they do not align perfectly (Stanley, Markman, & Whitton, 2002).

- **Seek External Support:** Consider relationship education programs or therapy to guide couples in navigating differing life compasses (Hawkins, Blanchard, Baldwin, & Fawcett, 2008).

- **Strengthen Communication Skills:** Enhance the ability to discuss and negotiate different viewpoints without escalating conflicts (Halford, Markman, & Stanley, 2008).

Reflective Prompts

Finally, here are three questions to ask yourself to align core values and goals in your marriage:

1. **Core Beliefs and Aspirations:** Delve deep into your core beliefs and aspirations. Are there values you hold dear that your partner might not fully understand or vice versa? Initiate open conversations to bridge any gaps in understanding and find common ground.

2. **Compromise and Collaborate:** Think about moments where differing values led to conflicts. How can both of you foster a spirit of compromise and collaboration, valuing the relationship over the need to be "right"?

3. **Respect and Appreciation:** Reflect on how you show respect and appreciation for your partner's values, even when they differ from yours. Finding ways to acknowledge and celebrate these differences can enrich the relationship.

_____

_____

_____

_____

_____

_____

CHAPTER 7

Family Pressures

Navigating Relations, Strengthening Ties

The chatter of family voices filled the living room and kitchen. Every summer, Chaquela and Denzel hosted a family reunion at their home, a tradition they both cherished. However, the undercurrents of unsolicited advice and judgments had become increasingly difficult to navigate.

Denzel's mother, Eleanor, cornered Chaquela in the kitchen. "You know, Chaquela, if you made more homemade meals, maybe Denzel wouldn't work late so often," she hinted with a fake smile. Chaquela noticed that after all these years, she was still called by her name, not "dear" or "honey," as the wives of Denzel's brothers were referred to.

Chaquela forced a polite nod, biting back a retort. This was not the first time Eleanor had insinuated her shortcomings as a wife.

But later, Chaquela overheard her father lecturing Denzel on the merits of financial investments, questioning his decision to start a small business. "It is risky, Denzel. You need to think about your family's future."

The day wore on, and the unsolicited opinions piled up, causing tension to simmer beneath the surface. That night, after the last guest had departed, Chaquela and Denzel collapsed on the couch, emotionally drained.

"This is our life, our marriage, our choices, and yes, our parents," Chaquela whispered, frustration evident in her voice. "Why can't they see the hurt they cause with their words?"

Denzel sighed, grabbing one of his long dreadlocks for support. "It is hard, I know. They mean well, but..."

"But we need boundaries," Chaquela finished.

They sat silently, realizing the importance of protecting their relationship from external pressures. While family was essential, so was the sanctity of their shared life. It was time to set some limits while maintaining the bonds of love and respect.

Setting the Stage

Family, often described as the bedrock of society, serves as our first introduction to relationships, love, trust, and understanding. Yet, as comforting as the embrace of a family can be, it can also exert pressures and present challenges, especially within the bounds of marital unions. When two individuals marry, it is not just a union of two souls but also a merging of two families, each with its dynamics, traditions, expectations, and histories.

From the beginning of courtship, family expectations can weigh heavily on couples. Family pressures can also introduce complexities into a relationship, whether the subtle nudging toward certain traditions or more overt demands regarding lifestyle choices. Over time, as marital roles are defined, external influences from family can challenge a couple's autonomy, sometimes even dictating decisions or driving wedges between partners.

In this chapter, we venture into the intricate web of family pressures within marital relationships. We will explore how external expectations can support and strain the bond and how couples can navigate the fine line between honoring their familial ties while safeguarding their unique relationship.

As we tread this path, readers will be invited to reflect on how family influences play out in their relationships. The journey aims to empower couples with strategies to recognize, address, and manage family pressures, emphasizing the importance of setting boundaries, ensuring clear communication, and nurturing a relationship that, while respectful of family ties, remains true to its unique essence and priorities.

First and foremost, let's ground ourselves in the research associated with this topic.

In-depth Research Dive

The influence of family pressures on marital relationships has been a significant area of exploration in family psychology. According to Bradbury, Fincham, and Beach (2000), the expectations and intrusions from extended family members can significantly increase stress in marital relationships. Trust and intimacy can erode when partners perceive their spouse as not adequately shielding them from family pressures. Couples with neither rigid nor permeable boundaries experienced higher marital satisfaction, emphasizing the importance of establishing clear, flexible limitations with extended family.

Cultural and societal norms play a profound role in shaping marital dynamics. Research by Chung (2007) illuminated the challenges faced by couples who bridge two different cultural worlds. In multicultural marriages, the partners often experience intensified family pressures in the form of traditional expectations and norms. When there is incongruence between the couple's desired marital role and the expectations of their families, it can lead to chronic marital discord. Furthermore, the importance of unity in partners' views on their roles in the face of external family pressure was a robust predictor of marital satisfaction.

Financial obligations, intertwined with family pressures, can act as a significant strain on marriages. A study by Dew, Britt, and Huston (2012) revealed that financial disagreements were stronger predictors of divorce than other common marital disagreements. Interestingly, not just the presence of debt creates strain, but the reasons behind that debt can significantly damage the relationship. Debts incurred from family pressures, such as aiding family members or pursuing status symbols to gain family approval, were particularly contentious and detrimental to marital health.

The pressure to prioritize career or family, often influenced by external family voices, can introduce unique challenges. According to Nomaguchi and Milkie (2003), marital satisfaction was at risk when spouses experienced role overload, often resulting from trying to meet work and family demands. Particularly, when one partner felt external pressure to prioritize work while the other was inclined toward familial roles, the resultant role conflict and overload significantly compromised marital quality.

Parental involvement in the lives of married couples can be both a blessing and a source of contention. According to Fingerman (2001), while parental support can offer emotional and sometimes financial relief to couples, it can also become a source of external pressure, especially if the help comes with strings attached or implicit expectations. Such expectations could influence decisions about child-rearing practices, home purchases, or career choices. The study concluded that when couples perceive these interventions as overly intrusive or misaligned with their shared goals, it can amplify marital conflict.

Another dimension of family pressures arises from the interplay of family-of-origin influences and individual partner differences. A study by Amato and Rogers (1997) delved into the negative spillover effects of parental marital quality on their offspring's relationships. They found that individuals who witnessed frequent parental conflicts during their formative years often carried residual anxieties and conflict patterns into their marriages. These imprinted behaviors and external family pressures can potentiate discord and dissatisfaction in marital relationships.

Role expectations, particularly in the context of gender, present another complexity in understanding family pressures on marriages. Eagly, Wood, and Diekman (2000) highlighted that societal norms and familial expectations often delineate distinct roles for husbands and wives. While some couples comfortably fit into these traditional roles, others might find them restrictive or incongruent with their aspirations. When one or both partners feel trapped or stifled by roles that do not align with their identity or aspirations, it can intensify resentment and misunderstanding.

A significant part of navigating family pressures is the ability of the couple to communicate and present a united front. According to Gottman and Levenson (2000), couples who succeed in cultivating a shared meaning system – encompassing shared values, symbols, and rituals – are better equipped to buffer their relationship against external stresses, including family pressures. This collective narrative becomes their anchor, enabling them to negotiate external pressures more effectively and minimizing potential rifts in the marital relationship.

Reflections and Insights

The Impact of External Expectations: Family Pressures and Organizational Dynamics

I've been privy to a broad spectrum of employee mindsets throughout my career. As a senior leader, my journey has been punctuated by observations and interactions that gave me a window into the potent influence of family pressures on individual aspirations and performance. Comparing this influence to the dynamics of marriage reveals striking similarities; just as in a union where external forces can strain the bond, in a business setting, external familial expectations can impact an individual's contentment and alignment with the organization's objectives.

While in the bus industry, I came across various colleagues who boasted about their family backgrounds. These individuals frequently mentioned their parents' professions, their grandparents' educational accomplishments, and the successes of their siblings in different fields. Such disclosures made me ponder the environment in which these individuals were nurtured. Was the conversation at their dinner tables about upholding family legacies and matching up to their ancestors' achievements?

This persistent emphasis on familial success stories illustrated a pattern. These individuals were not just propelled by personal ambition but bore the weight of living up to their family's expectations. Such pressures seemed to fuel their assertiveness in seeking political influence and striving for the highest salaries. On one hand, they appeared to be driven by personal aspirations and on the other side, they were after a quest for familial validation and respect.

In contrast, I encountered what I term "corporate citizens." These individuals frequently expressed dissatisfaction with their roles, always had concerns, and often occupied lower rungs in the organization's hierarchy. However, their contentment stemmed from a different source. They derived satisfaction from providing for their families rather than seeking leadership positions or a more significant status. Their primary motivation wasn't climbing the corporate ladder but ensuring a stable livelihood for their loved ones.

Reflecting on these two sets of employees made me realize an essential truth: the aspirations and expectations set outside the organization – by families, society, and personal networks – significantly influence how individuals operate within the organization. Both categories, whether driven by the extrinsic motivation to uphold family legacies or intrinsically motivated by the desire to provide for their families, come with external pressures.

Drawing parallels with marriage, just as a couple might feel content in their bond, an employee might be perfectly satisfied in their role within the organization. Yet, tensions arise if external pressures – from families or societal norms – dictate a different path or instill a sense of inadequacy. When introduced into the "organizational family," these external pressures can create discord and misalignment of goals.

In both scenarios, acknowledging and navigating these external pressures is crucial, whether it's a marriage or an organization. Only by understanding and addressing these influences can one truly find balance, fulfillment, and a harmonious dynamic, whether in a marital union or an organizational structure.

Crossing the Line: When Family Expectations Challenge Corporate and Marital Integrity

When we discuss external influences on one's corporate commitments, some scenarios, though they may seem exaggerated, vividly illustrate the depths to which these pressures can go. Consider the case of an individual employed at a fast-food joint, such as McDonald's. This person constantly faces family members dropping by, each expecting free food and leveraging their familial connection. Such a situation compromises the individual's integrity and puts them in a precarious position with their employer.

Taking this theme further, I'm reminded of a film I once saw. It depicted the story of a woman working at a bank who later became the robbery target. As the plot unravels, she discovers, much to her horror, that her cousin was involved in the heist. Here, the narrative delves deep into the dilemma of blood ties versus ethical duty. The protagonist grapples with the intense family pressure revolving around loyalty and the age-old adage of whether "blood is thicker than water." Would she prioritize her family ties over her duty to the bank and the law? Thankfully, despite the heart-wrenching turmoil, she chooses the path of righteousness. However, the weight of that familial expectation and the immense pressure it exerted on her was palpable.

These instances underscore families' profound influence over one's professional life. Yet, this doesn't just stop at one's career. Such pressures can potentially seep into personal spaces, especially marital relationships. The intense dilemma of choosing between family loyalty and professional or moral duty can strain a marriage's foundational trust and understanding. I can't claim immunity from such challenges, either. As we delve further, I'll share a more personal and extreme example that showcases how these pressures threatened the stability of my marriage, drawing parallels to how the earlier examples endangered the job security and reputational integrity of those individuals and their respective organizations.

Family Pressures and Finding Strength in Unlikely Places

The foundation upon which Bonita and I have built our relationship is rooted not in grand celebrations or community encouragement but in overcoming personal struggles and finding strength in unexpected corners.

When Bonita entered my life, our shared experiences became our strength. Neither of us had experienced family pressures to excel or maintain a marriage. Our mantra became clear: learn from the past, not emulate it. Our parents might have loved us, but we aimed to break the cycle and provide a contrasting backdrop for our children. It might seem like an unorthodox recipe for success, but the results have made our story worth sharing.

Yet, still, Bonita, much like me, had her set of challenges. She hailed from a background that did not exactly lay out the red carpet of expectations. For us, the absence of pressure from our families to succeed was both a blessing and a curse. It allowed us to chart our course without the weight of expectations, but it also meant there was no roadmap to guide us or benchmarks to measure up to.

During our early days of dating, we would sit in my car outside a nightclub where I was performing and awaiting the next set. We shared tales of our tumultuous pasts. "You know," Bonita would often say, her eyes reflecting the look of a woman who has never had the opportunity to have it easy in life, as she was working two jobs, "maybe it's a good thing that we don't have these big family pressures. It means we can write our story without anyone telling us what to do."

At least, that is what we thought.

Interwoven Threads:
The Familial Tensions that Shaped Our Unity

While it might seem from the outside that Bonita and I stepped into matrimony free from the burdens of familial intricacies, our union revealed latent and complex dynamics. These pressures, often subtle yet profound, presented unexpected challenges.

In the developing phase of our marriage, a hidden tension bubbled between Bonita and my sister, Raschunda. Although I was oblivious to its origins, it became clear that misunderstandings and misconceptions were marring their relationship. Having been privy to my past relationships, Raschunda became overly protective, casting a wary eye on Bonita. This caution, stemming from a genuine concern for my well-being, inadvertently made Bonita feel cornered and judged.

Bonita, too, introduced her family dynamics into our marriage. She shared a deep bond with her older sister, Charlotte, often seeking her wisdom and counsel. At first, I struggled with this dependency, hoping Bonita would lean on our relationship more. However, understanding the gravity of their bond, shaped by the tragic loss of their mother, I grew empathetic. Charlotte had become a beacon of strength and support in Bonita's life, a role I learned to respect.

Our backgrounds, filled with their unique challenges, surprisingly resonated. Bonita spoke of her mother's formidable influence despite her deafness and how their family faced challenges, particularly given their father's multiple relationships. My family story bore similar scars. My parents parted ways early on, with revelations about my father's other relationships emerging much later. These familial complexities unexpectedly bridged our understanding, drawing us closer.

Outside judgments, too, played their role. Our families faced external scrutiny, with some relatives casting us in diminished, needy roles. These labels, however, only served to galvanize our familial bonds. Just as Raschunda and I stood united, so did Bonita with her siblings, forging an unyielding front against societal judgments.

Reflecting on these familial dynamics, I discerned the value of discernment in addressing issues. It's not always necessary to vocalize every concern; some are rooted more in personal perceptions than reality. For instance, Bonita chose to keep her interactions with Raschunda from me until two decades into our relationship. While these challenges were genuine, they reminded me that not every issue needs immediate resolution. Time, patience, and faith can sometimes offer the clarity we seek.

In hindsight, immediate confrontations might have been premature. Our journey as a couple, filled with understanding and effective communication, was paramount. While Bonita gradually saw Raschunda warm up to her, I began to appreciate Charlotte's protective stance. Both were merely big sisters doing what big sisters do.

While Bonita and I navigated the woven complexities of our intertwined families, my history bore witness to even deep-rooted tensions. With the theme of familial challenges fresh in our minds, it's important to delve into the crucible that shaped the woman who raised me.

Layers of Resilience: A Glimpse into My Mother's Past

At the age of 21, my mother embarked on motherhood. Life had already dealt her profound blows: the devastating loss of her mother, Pearlie Mae, to cancer two years prior and the unspeakable pain of losing two siblings at birth in a mere span of five years. Her world was shadowed with grief, making her journey into a new relationship all the more challenging.

Entering a union with my father, she hoped for a respite, a fresh chapter. Instead, she was trapped in a tumultuous relationship marred by my father's abusive tendencies. But in life's darkest moments, glimmers of hope often appear. In pure generosity, my grandmother, Lillie Mae, offered them land on her farm, envisioning a sanctuary for my sister, Raschunda, my mother, my father, and me.

Yet, hope was fleeting. My mother made a courageous decision in less than a year, burdened by my father's escalating abuse, his troubling brushes with the law, and a trail of infidelities. With a toddler and another young child by her side, she sought refuge in Dallas, hoping to rewrite her narrative.

But fate had another twist. My father followed her to the city and, to add salt to her wounds entered a relationship with her close relative. This series of events, paired with the baggage of her past, started to wear down her mental resilience. Hospitalizations for psychiatric care became frequent. On some nights, she battled inner demons so fierce they made her contemplate the unthinkable.

To the outside world, my mother was a beacon of talent. Her soulful Gospel-singing voice, intellect, and the love she elicited from those who truly knew her masked the scars she hid. Stories whispered in hushed tones told of a fiercely protective woman who would confront and even resort to violence if anyone threatened her family.

Unfortunately, violence was a frequent visitor in the neighborhood my sister and I grew up in. But the environment at home, fueled by our mother's traumatic experiences, added a unique layer to our upbringing. Her clashes with my sister were often intense, their relationship a tumultuous mix of deep love and profound pain. A cycle of hurt, forgiveness, and reconciliation became a defining pattern in our home, culminating in a heart-wrenching incident on my wedding day.

Our Wedding Night: When Family Pressures Cast Shadows on New Beginnings

Our wedding day, meant to be the happiest day of our lives, became a stark testament to the destructive power of unchecked family pressures. The joy and anticipation were suddenly overshadowed when an unthinkable altercation occurred between my sister and mother, leading to my sister tragically shooting my mother.

As the reality of the incident began to set in, the weight of societal judgment and speculation pressed down on Bonita and me. Whispers echoed through the crowd: "Will they call off the wedding?" "Should he rush back to Dallas?" "What does this mean for their future?" Their voices, veiled in concern, sounded more like criticisms.

And for Bonita, the weight of being pregnant, of bringing a child into what others might see as a tumultuous family dynamic, seemed to amplify the scrutiny. Her decision was open to judgment in their eyes: "Is he the right partner, especially after such a family incident?"

But in that moment of deafening doubt, Bonita and I found clarity in the simplest gestures: She took my hand. An unspoken promise passed between us. Our love needed its sanctuary, insulated from the surrounding chaos. Rather than rushing to the hospital or police station, we went home, allowing ourselves to grieve, process, and find solace in each other.

Amidst the backdrop of our wedding's unfortunate turn and society's relentless scrutiny, I found myself battling mental and emotional turmoil. And just as the pressures seemed unbearable, we were blessed with our son's arrival, bringing joy and a fresh wave of anxiety. My role shifted overnight from a new husband grappling with a family tragedy to a father striving to protect his child from the shadows of our past.

However, despite her physical and emotional wounds, my mother showed up shortly after his birth, her jaw a testament to the incident's severity. One cherished photograph from that time captures a serene moment: my son, Tyler, resting on my mother's wounded heart. It encapsulated hope, resilience, and love amidst adversity.

Yet, underlying the joy and warmth in that photo was an inescapable void. My sister and mother were absent from our wedding album and this intimate snapshot. While practical reasons like my sister's military duty accounted for her absence at Tyler's birth, the emotional vacuum was about more than mere presence. I had dreamt of that emblematic family photograph – a captured moment of unity with my mother, sister, son, and myself during life's monumental phases. Even years later, the persistent absence in those frames remains a stark reflection of the challenges we endured and the familial bond we yearned to restore.

From Turmoil to Triumph: Navigating the Universal Complexities of Family Dynamics

The year that followed the tragic incident was rife with emotional turbulence, placing me often at the intersection of conflicting roles – the mediator, the healer, and the peacemaker. Trying to mend the fractured bond between my mother and sister often felt like navigating a ship through a relentless storm.

Yet, an unexpected beacon of hope emerged during this familial chaos: the younger generation. About two years into this storm, I observed my sister's subtle gestures of reconciliation by entrusting our mother with the care of her son, Rashad. Though seemingly ordinary, these moments bore testament to silent conversations of forgiveness and second chances. It was as if the children, in their innocence, were mending the broken bridges, reminding us of the inherent healing power of family bonds.

While I felt isolated in my struggles, Bonita's presence reminded me of unity and shared responsibility.

Over time, through shared moments, prayers, and unwavering patience, our family tapestry, once torn, started to mend. This process culminated in the joyful celebration of my sister's wedding a decade later. Witnessing my mother's glowing pride as she celebrated her daughter's union was a poignant testament to our journey from despair to jubilation.

Every family wrestles with shadows from the past and societal pressures, highlighting the transformative nature of such challenges. Each family has unique challenges, from dramatic sagas to subtler yet profound struggles.

Religion

Religion, with its deeply entrenched beliefs and customs, is often a significant source of family pressure, especially when partners come from different faith backgrounds. Such differences, whether from cultural, traditional, or doctrinal origins, can precipitate challenges in decisions that affect the family unit, be it child-rearing, holiday celebrations, or even seemingly trivial matters like choosing where to reside.

Religion was no stranger to introducing tension in Bonita's and my life. My father, a Pentecostal pastor, believed in personal communion with God, spiritual gifts, and vibrant, expressive worship. Conversely, his six siblings, Jehovah's Witnesses, held different convictions, encompassing unique doctrines about God and Jesus, celebrations, and specific religious observances.

While tacitly acknowledged, these differences often loomed large in family gatherings, like a silent yet insistent "elephant in the room." Everyone tiptoed around it, but the divergence was palpable and unavoidable.

The stark contrast between our religious backgrounds was painfully evident during my grandmother Lillie Mae's funeral. As my father stepped forward to honor her memory with a eulogy, a segment of the family excused themselves from the sanctuary due to their Jehovah's Witness beliefs. This wasn't just a matter of personal choice; it embodied their deep-rooted convictions against participating in non-aligned religious rituals. Such instances underscored the unspoken chasms within our family fabric.

Recognizing these undercurrents, Bonita and I strived to build bridges where we could. A cherished tradition during family dinners – the pre-meal prayer – transformed into a testament to our commitment to inclusivity. Instead of a conventional prayer, we introduced a silent reflection, saying, "Let's have a moment of silence. If you want to pray, please do so. If not, take a moment to reflect."

This change wasn't just about prayer and respecting and valuing the myriad beliefs that constituted our family mosaic. In these small gestures, we hoped to foster an environment where every faith felt acknowledged, every person felt respected, and every difference was celebrated.

Interracial and Intercultural Marriages

Interracial and intercultural marriages amalgamate distinct cultures, customs, and values, offering a rich tapestry of experiences. While these unions present a vibrant mosaic of backgrounds, they also come with unique challenges. The blending of traditions can be enlightening and complex, as partners often carry familial and societal expectations. Success in such relationships hinges on open communication, mutual respect, and embracing each other's heritage.

For many in such unions, there's an added layer of depth, a profound necessity for conversations that might not arise in monoculture relationships. For instance, a Black man like Tyler marrying Tegan, a white woman, has to introduce discussions about racial disparities, societal perceptions, and the weight of systemic biases. These conversations are paramount, encompassing topics like policing, racial profiling, and the shared history of racial tensions. Such discussions aren't mere abstract debates but pivotal realities that could impact their daily lives and future children's lives.

However, it's essential to recognize that these conversations also provide an invaluable opportunity. By navigating these intricacies together, Tyler and Tegan strengthen their bond and enrich their understanding of the world. Their union becomes a living testament to the transformative power of love that bridges cultural divides.

As parents, Bonita and I find profound admiration in their journey. Watching Tyler and Tegan meld their worlds, embracing the beauty and the challenges of their distinct backgrounds, affirms love's power. Their proactive approach to discussing hard-hitting issues, from systemic racism to cultural nuances, showcases their commitment to building a resilient foundation for their relationship.

Our family has seen the remarkable tapestry of love in various forms, underlining that genuine connections surpass societal barriers. Interracial and intercultural unions bring forth the poignant lesson that love transcends boundaries. When navigated with understanding and respect, these relationships can serve as torchbearers, illuminating the path to a more inclusive and understanding world.

Political Beliefs and Family Pressures

In any relationship, introducing the topic of politics can be akin to lighting a match in a dry forest. Each political belief, policy stance, or voting decision often intertwines with core values, personal experiences, and one's societal vision. When partners hold opposing political views, these differences can become a hotbed for passionate debates, misunderstandings, and sometimes deep-rooted animosities.

Within the sprawling vastness of Texas, where a rich tapestry of cultures, backgrounds, and beliefs converge, navigating political conversations requires an intricate dance. This is especially true when personal connections cross party lines.

Bonita and I have always prioritized fostering an environment where everyone feels empowered to express their opinions, regardless of their political affiliation. Yet, we also recognize the divisive nature of politics in the present climate. Thus, while our home is a haven of openness, we often counsel our children to be cautious and considerate when discussing politics in larger circles, aware of the rifts such differences can create.

The dynamic political landscape has evolved significantly over the years. Not too long ago, political disagreements, while passionate, rarely severed ties. People could engage in spirited debates but still maintain a foundation of mutual respect. Fast-forward to today, the divisive rhetoric and deep-seated animosities between opposing political camps have added a layer of complexity to interpersonal relationships. Bonita and I have witnessed close friends who once celebrated their differences become estranged due to the changing political atmosphere. Their bonds, once unshakeable, became brittle in the face of contentious policy debates and the charged sociopolitical climate.

One significant factor is that today's political beliefs often intersect with broader societal issues such as race, gender identity, immigration, and other polarizing topics. Thus, a disagreement isn't merely about a candidate or a policy; it can delve into personal experiences and identities.

For couples, this underscores the necessity of fostering open channels of communication. Even if they hail from different political spectrums, understanding and respecting each other's viewpoints is crucial. By setting boundaries, such as avoiding combative rhetoric or dedicating specific times for constructive discussions, couples can navigate these treacherous waters, ensuring that political beliefs enhance rather than undermine their relationship.

Navigating the Labyrinth: The Interplay of Family Pressures in Marriages

Underneath familial celebrations are subtle tensions and pressures that can sometimes overshadow the joy of family bonds.

Differences, whether in terms of cultural backgrounds, religious beliefs, or political affiliations, can play dual roles in a marriage. They can serve as bridges, offering opportunities for couples to learn, grow, and enrich their shared experience. However, these differences can become walls in the absence of open communication and mutual respect, casting shadows of misunderstanding and mistrust.

In navigating familial pressures, love remains the key, consistently showcasing its potential to heal and uplift. While external pressures are a reality, every couple has the power to shape their narrative. By recognizing the challenges, fostering open dialogue, and drawing strength from their shared journey, couples can craft a story that is uniquely theirs, celebrating their individuality and shared experiences.

Strategies for Improvement

The fabric of family is woven with emotions, expectations, and histories that can sometimes pull at the seams of a marriage. While the family forms an essential support system, their dynamics can introduce external stresses into the marital equation. From differences in upbringing to varying familial values, these pressures can magnify marital discord if not addressed.

Couples must stand united, forging a bond that respects the influences of extended family while prioritizing their marital unit. Transparent communication, establishing clear boundaries, and mutual respect can assist couples in navigating these familial waters, ensuring that the marriage remains steady amidst external waves.

While external family pressures can be challenging, it is not insurmountable. A healthy marriage can weather these pressures with the right strategies. Grounded in empirical research, here are several tactics couples can employ to minimize the negative impacts of family pressures:

1. **Establish Clear Boundaries:** Creating firm boundaries with extended family members can help shield your relationship from undue influence (Papp, Cummings, & Goeke-Morey, 2002).

2. **Unified Front:** Presenting decisions and viewpoints as a unified team can deter family members from driving a wedge between partners (Kellas, LeClair-Underberg, & Normand, 2018).

3. **Prioritize Marital Concerns:** Ensure your partner's feelings and concerns are prioritized above external family demands (Cowan & Cowan, 2000).

4. **Open Dialogue:** Discuss family pressures openly with your partner to understand and respect each other's perspectives (Curran, Hazen, Jacobvitz, & Feldman, 2005).

5. **Seek Neutral Mediation:** If family pressures escalate, consider seeking family therapy or counseling to facilitate effective communication (Walsh, 2016).

6. **Cultural Respect:** Understand and respect the cultural norms that might influence family pressures while finding a balanced approach that suits both partners (Farver, Narang, & Bhadha, 2002).

Reflective Prompts

Finally, here are three questions to ask yourself to minimize the effect of family pressures in your marriage:

1. **Setting Boundaries:** Consider past instances where family involvement or opinions caused tension in your relationship. How can you jointly establish boundaries to protect your relationship while maintaining family ties?

2. **Unified Front:** Reflect on how you and your partner handle external pressures. Are there moments when one of you feels unsupported? Discuss strategies to present a unified front in family situations, ensuring both voices are heard and valued.

3. **Understanding and Empathy:** Family dynamics and histories vary. How often do you take time to understand your partner's family background and its impact on them? Showing empathy and understanding can make navigating family pressures smoother for both of you.

CHAPTER 8

Work and Career Pressures

Harmonizing Career and Home

The city skyline painted a tale of ambition as the evening sun set, casting long shadows that seemed to mirror the shifting dynamics within one household. Marcus had always been the cornerstone, his stable corporate role providing both security and a certain status. With pride, he had always carried the title of primary breadwinner.

But the landscape changed when Kara's tech startup, once a mere side hustle, started making headlines. The accolades and financial milestones began to pour in, and with every success Kara enjoyed, a latent tension began to brew.

One evening, a glossy magazine with Kara's poised figure on the cover caught Marcus's eye. "Entrepreneur of the Year," it proclaimed. While pride swelled in him, an unfamiliar sting of envy lurked.

Sensing his turmoil, Kara approached, "It feels like we're competing, doesn't it?"

He exhaled, "I've been the provider, and now with all this, I feel... a bit sidelined."

Kara, trying to tread gently, replied, "My accomplishments don't diminish yours, Marcus. We should be celebrating together."

"But it's changed things," he admitted, his voice a mere whisper, "It feels like there's a shift in our balance."

A pause filled the room before Kara spoke, her voice tinged with concern, "I wish you'd talked about this sooner."

He looked at her earnestly, "It took me a while to understand my feelings."

As they intertwined their fingers, there was an unsaid commitment to journey through this new chapter together. However, in the recesses of her mind, Kara wondered, "What else has he been keeping from me? I supported his success. Now he is questioning mine?" Their bond was strong, but it was clear that open communication would be essential to navigate the challenges ahead.

Setting the Stage

*I*n today's fast-paced world, the demands of a career often pull individuals in myriad directions, acting as a beacon of personal achievement and at times, a strain on personal relationships. Balancing the weight of professional ambitions with the needs of a marital partnership presents its unique challenges. When two careers come into play, the dynamics become even more intricate, with job pressures, timings, relocations, and ambitions sometimes at odds with marital harmony.

Imagine the scenario: early morning rushes, missed dinners, late-night calls, and weekends dominated by emails. The relentless pursuit of professional success can create a chasm in marital connections, even among the most loving couples. Over time, this can lead to neglect, resentment, and isolation, with partners feeling more like passing ships than connected souls.

This chapter will delve into the multifaceted work and career pressures on marriages. We will explore the delicate balancing act required to juggle professional aspirations with the demands and desires of a marital partnership. More than just understanding the challenges, the aim is to uncover strategies for couples to ensure their bond remains strong, even in the face of professional demands.

As we navigate this topic, it becomes evident that a conscious effort is needed to ensure that the fire of love does not overshadow the spark of ambition. With mutual understanding, open dialogue, and a shared vision for the future, couples can build a thriving relationship, celebrating individual successes and shared milestones.

A review of the relevant research is a good starting point.

In-Depth Research Dive

According to Greenhaus and Beutell (1985), work-life conflict occurs when work and personal life demands are incompatible, making it difficult for individuals to fulfill responsibilities in both domains. This conflict can manifest as time-based, where physical presence is required in two places simultaneously, or strain-based, where stress in one role impedes performance in another. Their research suggests that strain-based conflict, in particular, can erode marital satisfaction as partners bring workplace stress into their home lives, affecting the emotional atmosphere of the relationship.

A study by Frone, Russell, and Cooper (1992) delved into the reciprocal relationship between work-related stress and marital satisfaction. Their findings indicated that work-related stress negatively influences marital satisfaction, and marital discord can also increase job-related distress. This cyclical effect emphasizes the interconnected nature of work and personal life, with disturbances in one area spilling over into the other, potentially creating a vicious cycle that can challenge the stability of a marriage.

Eby, Casper, Lockwood, Bordeaux, and Brinley (2005) explored the role of work overload and its relation to marital dissatisfaction. Their findings showed that spouses who experience high levels of work overload, which involves working long hours or having an excessive workload, often face challenges in meeting family responsibilities. The inability to be present and contribute to household and familial duties can create feelings of guilt, leading to marital strain. It highlights the importance of shared responsibility and understanding in supporting both partners.

Ensuring proper boundaries between work and personal life is a proactive step toward preserving marital harmony. Kossek, Noe, and DeMarr (1999) investigated the effects of boundary management strategies on marital satisfaction. Their research showed that couples who actively manage and negotiate their work-life boundaries, prioritizing family events and ensuring that work does not consistently infringe upon personal time tend to report higher levels of marital satisfaction. This emphasizes the significance of open dialogue and mutual respect in balancing the dual demands of career and matrimonial responsibilities.

A study by Nomaguchi (2009) delved into the complexities of perceived imbalances between work and personal life. The study highlighted that individuals often assess work-life balance not merely by the quantity of time dedicated to each domain but by the quality of interactions and experiences within each realm. The research unveiled that spouse who felt they had meaningful, engaging interactions in their work and personal lives reported higher marital satisfaction, even when faced with long work hours. The research suggests that the narrative around work-life balance might need a more nuanced approach, focusing on time allocation and the value derived from the time spent.

Netemeyer, Boles, and McMurrian (1996) highlighted the concept of role overload as a significant contributor to work-family conflict. Their findings illuminated that when individuals perceive their workplace or home roles as too extensive or demanding, it often reduces role performance in both spheres. In marriage, when one partner experiences role overload, the ripple effects can lead to feelings of inadequacy, a lack of mutual support, and an increased vulnerability to conflict. Such dynamics underscore the importance of partners maintaining a continuous dialogue about their roles, capacities, and feelings, ensuring mutual understanding and support.

Work flexibility has emerged as a potential antidote to the challenges of work and career pressures. According to Hill, Erickson, Holmes, and Ferris (2010), couples with at least one partner who has access to flexible work arrangements often exhibit higher marital satisfaction. Their research suggests that such flexibility empowers couples to adapt to each other's schedules, prioritize family activities, and ensure mutual participation in work and personal life. This adaptability, in turn, fosters a sense of collaboration, mutual support, and understanding, crucial elements for marital stability.

Finally, a research project by Amstad, Meier, Fasel, Elfering, and Semmer (2011) discussed the concept of spillover and crossover effects in the context of work and family. Spillover refers to the transfer of mood and behaviors from one domain (like work) to another (like family), while crossover implies the transfer of moods and behaviors between partners. The study discovered that negative spillovers, such as bringing work stress home, can intensify marital conflict. On the other hand, positive spillovers, like sharing achievements and joyous moments from work, can enhance marital intimacy. It underscores the role of awareness in mitigating negative spillovers and amplifying positive ones, emphasizing the importance of being mindful of what we bring into our marital space.

Reflections and Insights

Throughout my professional journey, I've faced numerous enticing opportunities. However, I've consistently chosen my family's well-being over greater professional accolades. The choices ranged from lucrative roles at tech giants like Microsoft in Seattle, leadership positions with Adobe, and strategic placements in marketing tech in San Jose or Chicago. Yet, at each crossroads, I've chosen the path that ensured my family's normalcy and well-being over a heftier paycheck. This decision was rooted not in fear but in a profound understanding of the value of presence.

Today, particularly in the black community, there's a pervasive narrative of achieving generational wealth "by any ethical means necessary." But often, this translates to individuals stretching themselves thin, juggling multiple jobs or side hustles to the detriment of their familial relationships. The quest for financial progress shouldn't come at the expense of personal connections.

As a senior executive, I've always championed an outcomes-based approach rather than a tactics-driven one. My philosophy isn't rooted in laxity but in trusting the capabilities of my team and recognizing the importance of work-life balance. Each individual's equilibrium differs, and my role was to ensure they found theirs.

A defining moment during a family trip underscored the importance of work-life balance for me. After a rapid growth phase at work, a personal incident reminded me of the essential balance between work and family. No sooner had I arrived at a waterpark that my non-internet cell phone – before iPhones – had ended in a pool of water. This accidental disconnection turned into a conscious decoupling from work, redirecting my entire focus to the family. Upon my return, it was clear that the leaders I'd entrusted had seamlessly handled operations. The company thrived in my absence. This experience was an epiphany, underscoring the need to unplug and trust in the systems and people we put in place.

From that pivotal moment, I promised that vacations would be sacred, free from work intrusions, and I'd extend the same courtesy to my team.

In life, as in business, finding a balance is pivotal. But it's crucial to understand that this balance is not static. Just as businesses evolve and adapt to changing environments, relationships, too, require recalibrations and adjustments. Much like a thriving business, a successful marriage necessitates recognizing these shifts and making the necessary tweaks to ensure harmony and progress.

Redefining Roles: Unexpected Sacrifices and Career Changes

One particular Sunday morning, the house echoed with the usual hustle and bustle. My wife, Bonita, had already left for her job, where she was carving a name for herself as the Deli Manager at a local grocery store. Meanwhile, my daughter and I were planning to head to church. Music, after all, wasn't just my passion; it was my calling. As the church's musician, Sundays held a special significance.

But life has a way of throwing curveballs. As we prepared our young son Tyler for the outing, we noticed the heat radiating off his forehead. A fever. Concerned but not wanting to overreact, I suggested a quick bath might help lower his temperature. But the contrast between the tub's water and his feverish skin proved too much, and the unimaginable occurred. Tyler started having a febrile seizure, his little eyes rolling back, his body convulsing.

Panic surged through me. Grabbing Tyler, I shouted to my daughter to jump in the truck, and we sped towards the nearest hospital. In the chaos, we tried reaching Bonita, desperate for the calming presence she always provided. But every call went unanswered. She was probably helping a customer.

The emergency staff at the hospital immediately sensed the gravity of the situation and jumped into action. Minutes felt like hours, each second an eternity until a doctor finally emerged. Tyler was stable, he said, but they would transfer him to a specialized children's hospital. The relief of knowing he was okay was quickly followed by the doctor's remark about my state of dress. In the frenzy, I had rushed to the hospital in nothing more than a t-shirt and underwear.

Rushing back home to change, I returned to find Bonita at the hospital. A coworker had informed her and dropped her off, her face etched with worry but grateful that Tyler was recovering.

Over the next week, after the tumult had settled and Tyler was safely home getting back to his normal self, Bonita and I found ourselves in quiet conversation. That day's events had put into stark relief the fragility of life and the need for support.

The air in the room grew thick as we delved deeper into the topic of our family's future. As I reflected on the stability of my job and the passion I felt for it, I couldn't help but think about Bonita's journey, which was steeped in a rich tapestry of hard work and determination. Growing up, she'd always held down two jobs and helped her father tend to his fields of roses and produce. The notion of not working, of not being in the fray, was alien to her. She had an embedded sense of responsibility, not just to her family but to herself.

I watched her, wringing her hands, clearly struggling with the implications of our conversation. "I've always been independent, always earned my way," Bonita began, her voice quivering but firm. "Not heading out to work every day, not having my own income... what does that even mean? How would I buy you gifts for special occasions? What would my days look like?"

Her words resonated deeply. The decision before us wasn't merely about who would earn the bread or who would stay home; it was a fundamental shift in the dynamics of our partnership and a reassessment of our individual identities. I understood her apprehensions. Pausing her career wasn't just about hitting the pause button on a job; it was pressing pause on a significant part of who she was.

"Bonita," I began, "I realize that this decision isn't just about adjusting to a new life. I've seen the sacrifices you've made, your dedication, and the pride you take in working. It is all you have known. But we need to think long term, as I had to consider what could have happened and I know you do too. I may be over-reacting, but this is a time for us to try something different. I don't know how you staying at home works either, but we can now afford it. Let's try it out."

The weight of societal pressures, especially on women, is profound. The very essence of work and career pressures isn't just about the stresses of the job but also the decisions one has to make in light of unforeseen circumstances. For Bonita, it wasn't just about managing work-life balance, it was about grappling with societal expectations. Men were often seen as the providers, while women, despite making strides in their careers, were still expected to be the primary caregivers. This disparity and the intrinsic pressures it places on women are often understated.

She looked at me, eyes glistening, "This isn't just about Tyler's incident. But I want to do what is best for us all."

I nodded, "It's a life shift for you, more than for anyone else. And I deeply appreciate the sacrifice you're considering. I want you to know, Bonita, that pausing your career doesn't diminish your worth or contributions to this family. Our roles might change, but our partnership remains the same."

We sat in reflective silence. She was processing a multitude of feelings: guilt, pride, concern, and hope. A few moments later, she spoke, "I know we're doing this for the right reasons, but I need you to understand how big of a change this is for me."

"I do," I whispered. "And we'll navigate this together."

Bonita's decision to transition to a stay-at-home mom wasn't just a personal sacrifice; it was an acknowledgment of the broader pressures women face in their careers, especially when life throws unexpected challenges. The depth of such decisions is vast, often going beyond the surface-level understanding of roles and into the realm of identity, self-worth, and societal expectations.

Our journey in Texas was just beginning, but with it came profound realizations. While work and career pressures can encompass the challenges of the job, they can also pertain to the complexities of stopping one's career. Decisions like these are seldom easy, but with mutual respect, understanding, and a unified vision, couples can find their path, even amidst the most challenging crossroads.

Balancing Dual Careers After a Hiatus: Rediscovering Our Partnership Dynamics

In an era where families with two working parents are commonplace, Bonita and I have journeyed through varied stages in our relationship, each demanding unique adaptations and mutual understanding. Managing both professional aspirations and personal commitments is a reality faced by countless couples, and without careful attention, this balancing act can strain relationships.

Numerous studies highlight the challenges faced by dual-earning couples. For instance, Nomaguchi (2012) emphasized how professional obligations can significantly encroach upon personal time. This intrusion can result in diminished quality of shared moments, escalating disagreements over work-life balance, and even feelings of guilt or resentment regarding domestic roles (Matthews, Conger, & Wickrama, 1996). The tension caused by conflicting work and home responsibilities becomes especially prominent in couples where both partners are professionally active, leading to role strain (Eby et al., 2005).

As discussed earlier, at the beginning of our marriage, Bonita and I were part of the workforce. However, as we embraced parenthood and developed deeper trust and communication, we jointly decided Bonita would take on the invaluable role of a stay-at-home mom, a commitment that lasted two decades.

During this period, my career often took me away from home. The freedom and discretion in my senior leadership position meant spontaneous trips and the flexibility to change schedules at a moment's notice. For over two decades, this was our reality – I had the liberty to say, "Let's hit the road" or propose a sudden outing, and Bonita, ever the pillar of support, would seamlessly adapt. She'd prep, pack, and plan, ensuring our family's needs were met, all while setting aside her career aspirations. She enjoyed the vacation experiences we were able to provide for ourselves and our kids.

Yet, as time unfurled its changes and our children grew into their independence, Bonita, reinvigorated by a fresh sense of purpose, pursued and became a respiratory therapist. This transition wasn't just a return to the workforce; it was a rediscovery of a part of herself she had shelved for the sake of our family. With her re-entry, the dynamics of our relationship were thrust into uncharted territories. Suddenly, we found ourselves juggling two distinct career trajectories, each demanding its due respect and time.

The evolution of our professional lives brought along a sense of realization for me. No longer were the days when Bonita's schedule automatically aligned with mine. Her demanding 12-hour shifts, planned six weeks in advance, came with an inflexibility that we hadn't navigated before. Gone were the spontaneous trips; now, even a simple family event needed meticulous planning around her commitments. And the career pressures that we had largely evaded during our 25 years of marriage due to my fortunate position were considerations.

Still, through these new challenges, we held fast to the foundational practices that have always been the bedrock of our bond: shared meals, consistent communication, and treasured moments together. While my work travels have reduced, bringing me closer to home, the adjustments on my end have been significant.

If Bonita has to work on a holiday like Thanksgiving, our celebration shifts to a day that works around her time off. These adaptations have given me a firsthand appreciation of the struggles that dual-career couples face, especially when their lives are intertwined with children's schedules and activities. While Bonita and I have the luxury of now only coordinating with each other, the experience has been enlightening.

Now, the tables have turned. Just as Bonita once respected and adjusted to my unpredictable work rhythms, I've learned to adapt to hers, celebrating our shared journey and the mutual respect that continues to define our relationship. I aim to create an environment where Bonita feels no career pressures, mirroring the support and ease she once offered me.

Navigating Career Pressures in Dual-Earner Marriages

The complexities of managing dual careers within a marital relationship cannot be understated. In a world that increasingly demands both partners to juggle professional commitments with personal responsibilities, the inherent pressures can strain the very bonds that hold a couple together.

For the partner engrossed in long hours at work, there's a continuous challenge of balancing career pressures with familial responsibilities. This delicate act can often lead to feelings of being torn between two worlds: the immediate demands of a professional environment and the intimate moments at home that they might miss. While they strive for financial stability for the family, there's an underlying guilt of missing out on irreplaceable family memories. This conflict might manifest as a sense of detachment from their partner and children, possibly accompanied by a feeling that their relentless efforts aren't sufficiently acknowledged.

On the other hand, the partner who may have a more flexible schedule, or who shoulders a larger share of domestic responsibilities, grapples with a different kind of challenge. Their efforts, although less quantifiable in monetary terms, are vital for the family's well-being. Yet, there could be moments of self-doubt, of feeling less significant, or of yearning for greater appreciation for the often invisible tasks they undertake.

The intersection of these feelings, stemming from the stresses of their respective roles, can lead to miscommunication or even an emotional disconnect. Work pressures can blur the lines of understanding and appreciation, creating potential pitfalls where the relationship's foundation could tremble.

To navigate these potential landmines, a proactive approach rooted in empathy and mutual respect is vital. It's crucial for partners to acknowledge the dual nature of their roles and the unique challenges each faces. Appreciating the daily hurdles, whether it's a high-pressure meeting or managing a household crisis, becomes imperative.

Couples can find solace and strength by regularly validating each other's efforts, be it in the professional sphere or at home. Simple acts of gratitude, understanding the essence of mutual sacrifices, and investing time in discussing shared dreams and future aspirations can bridge the perceived gaps.

Amidst the unpredictability of careers and professional trajectories, Bonita and I have observed countless couples who commenced their marital journey with well-defined roles concerning work and finances. These roles often provided clarity and stability, but the volatility of the job market, unexpected shifts in roles, or professional relocations can test the very foundation of these agreements. The pressures arising from such work and career challenges often exacerbate the complexities of marital dynamics.

When confronted with these work-related curveballs, the initial shock can be daunting. The loss of steady income from a job or the upheaval caused by relocating for a job opportunity can strain not only the finances but also the emotional equilibrium of a relationship. These challenges, when combined with career pressures, can sometimes become a breeding ground for blame. It's an all too common scene: partners pointing fingers, assigning blame for decisions made or not made, lamenting over "what could have been" rather than focusing on "what can be done."

However, it's essential to remember that these challenges, while difficult, also present an opportunity: the chance for couples to rally together, unified against a common obstacle. The essence of partnership is collaboration, and it's during these trying times that true partnership shines. Instead of laying blame, couples can realign, reminding each other that they embarked on this journey as a team, and it's as a team that they'll find their way through.

Bonita and I firmly believe in the adage: "We entered this together; we'll navigate out of it together." It's an attitude that calls for mutual respect, understanding, and trust. It acknowledges that while not every partner can effortlessly reassure the other with "I've got this," every couple possesses the collective strength to devise a plan, adapt, and move forward.

In the face of work and career pressures, the focus should be less on the problem itself and more on how, as a united front, the couple can find solutions. The challenges might be external, but the strength to overcome them is deeply internal, rooted in the bond of the relationship. It's a testament to the resilience of couples who, when faced with work and career pressures, choose unity over division and collaboration over conflict.

Marital Competition: A Personal Reflection

Contrasted with unity and collaboration stands competition. In today's competitive landscape, success is often equated with financial earnings – a view that can potentially cloud the harmony within a marriage. While financial stability is undeniably crucial, undue emphasis on out-earning one's partner can lead to damaging rifts. For a relationship to thrive, both partners must prioritize unity over division and collaboration over competition.

The intricate web of this competition becomes clear when recalling my own past experience. Prior to tying the knot with Bonita, I dated someone during my college years. Our relationship ended when I faced challenges in securing my degree, leading to my initial departure from the institution. The separation was painful, and distance had grown between us. However, I still believed in the power of open communication and sought her input during a pivotal moment in my life.

Having started working as a planner for a bus company, a golden opportunity presented itself. I was awarded a fellowship, one that covered not just the completion of my undergraduate studies but also a doctoral program. The only stipulation was committing to a five-year tenure with the state.

Excited and hoping for her familiar perspective, I reached out to my ex-girlfriend. I'll never forget that conversation. The phone buzzed and her voice filled the silence. With enthusiasm, I relayed, "Hey, I've managed to get back on track. I've received a full fellowship to continue my education."

I expected words of encouragement, a shared excitement. Instead, her response was doused in skepticism. "How did you do that?" she queried, her voice laced with disbelief. I was taken aback. Her follow-up, "But you didn't graduate. What type of fellowship is that?" only deepened the sting.

It was in that crystallizing moment that I realized the depth of the divide. The distance between us wasn't just physical. She had always seen herself as the more accomplished partner and needed to maintain that dynamic. The idea of me potentially outshining her academic achievements was unsettling to her. This kind of competition, lurking in the shadows of a relationship, can be as corrosive as any external challenge. It's a competitive stance that is often clear before marriage but gets overlooked.

Competition extends beyond mere job titles; it also encompasses the rivalry in earnings.Tichenor (1999) and Kenney (2006) underscores the destabilizing impact when couples view their incomes competitively rather than as shared resources. Earnings competition can result in feelings of being undervalued or bearing a disproportionate share of financial responsibilities. Societal norms further muddy the waters, with Schwartz (1994) highlighting how society's gender expectations can heighten earnings-related marital tensions. As couples navigate this minefield, understanding and collaboration are paramount.

Fortunately, with Bonita, my journey has been starkly different. Our relationship has thrived on mutual respect, understanding, and the shared vision of lifting each other up. There's never been an underlying current of competition between us, career-wise or otherwise. And this has been a significant factor in the strength and resilience of our bond.

The specter of competition looms large in many relationships. When partners start to perceive each other as rivals rather than allies, it ushers in resentment, diminished support, and a subtle estrangement. This rivalry extends beyond career achievements, enveloping intellectual triumphs, social standing, and even the regard of peers or family members.

Addressing marital competition issues require a deep introspection and open dialogue. Partners must recognize and challenge any societal or self-imposed narratives that push them into competitive roles. Celebrating each other's successes, acknowledging vulnerabilities, and actively working towards a collaborative rather than competitive dynamic can be transformative.

It's pivotal for couples to understand that in the journey of life, they're co-pilots, not competitors in a race. Both have unique strengths and vulnerabilities, and the relationship thrives when these are synergized rather than juxtaposed.

Navigating Career Aspirations and Marital Fulfillment

In the dance of marriage, achieving synchrony between two dynamic careers poses an intricate challenge. For Bonita and me, the journey has been one of evolving roles, mutual respect, and a shared commitment to adaptability. While Bonita once sacrificed the thrum of a professional life for the haven of our home, the rhythm has shifted. As she returned to the demanding schedule of a respiratory therapist and I continued in a career with its own ebbs and flows, the spotlight was never on who took the lead, but rather on how we could best complement each other.

Work and career pressures, like most challenges in life, come with a dual potential: to pull apart or to bind tighter. The crux lies not in the external situations we encounter but in our internal responses to them. Do we let the embers of competition overshadow the warmth of companionship? Or do we acknowledge each other's aspirations and craft a shared narrative of success?

Bonita and I have witnessed many couples where disparity in earnings or the shadows of professional competition crept into the sanctity of their relationship. Yet, it's crucial to remember that the value of one's contribution to a marriage cannot – and should not – be measured by paychecks or professional accolades alone. In our partnership, we've learned to view our achievements, be they personal or professional, as collective victories. When I faced challenges, Bonita's wisdom was the perspective I sought; when she achieved milestones in her career, it was our shared joy.

However, it's essential to underscore that such a partnership doesn't materialize without effort. Regular, open communication has been our anchor. By discussing our aspirations, celebrating each other's achievements, and understanding the shifting demands of our careers, we've ensured that neither of us ever feels overshadowed or left behind.

Beyond communication, flexibility has been key. Just as we adapted our Thanksgiving celebrations when work called, we have molded our lives around the ever-changing contours of our professional lives, finding harmony in unpredictability.

In the grand mosaic of marriage, every piece – whether tinted by the hues of joy, challenges, compromises, or triumphs – has its place. Our careers have enriched this mosaic, adding depth and texture. Through it all, the lesson has been clear: while navigating career aspirations, it's the shared pursuit of marital fulfillment that truly charts the course.

Strategies for Improvement

Modern careers often blur the lines between professional and personal lives, overshadowing marital harmony. Commitments outside the home, vital for personal fulfillment, can overshadow nurturing marital ties. Balancing career and marriage is akin to walking a tightrope, where the weight of responsibilities must be carefully counterbalanced with the relationship's needs. Couples must recognize when work excessively tilts the balance, eventually leading to neglecting the duties at home.

Open dialogues about professional stresses and concerted efforts to allocate quality time can help restore equilibrium. By acknowledging the value of both spheres and ensuring neither eclipses the other, couples can cherish a union where love and ambition thrive side by side.

Balancing work and marital life are pivotal to the health and longevity of the relationship. Drawing from empirical studies, here are several approaches that couples can adopt to mitigate work and career pressures and their adverse effects on marriage:

- **Prioritize Quality Time:** Dedicate purposeful, uninterrupted time for each other irrespective of busy schedules, fostering intimacy and connection (Clark, 2000).

- **Negotiate Household Duties:** Sharing responsibilities can alleviate feelings of inequity and prevent resentment (Coltrane, 2000).

- **Practice Flexibility:** If feasible, consider flexible work arrangements, to accommodate family needs and priorities (Hill, Yang, Hawkins, & Ferris, 2004).

- **Implement Digital Detox:** Designate specific times when technology is off-limits to foster genuine connection and presence (Twenge & Campbell, 2018).

- **Discuss Work Stressors:** Open dialogue about work-related challenges can foster understanding and support (Rogers & May, 2003).

- **Engage in Joint Activities:** Participating in shared hobbies or activities can strengthen the marital bond and provide an escape from work pressures (Crawford, Houts, Huston, & George, 2002).

- **Seek Professional Guidance:** If work and career pressures persistently strain the marriage, couples therapy might offer constructive coping mechanisms (Doherty & Ryder, 2016).

Reflective Prompts

Finally, here are three questions to ask yourself to balance work and career in your marriage:

1. **Balancing Priorities:** Think about moments when work demands overshadowed relationship needs. How can you ensure a more balanced approach to prioritizing your career and relationship?

2. **Open Dialogue on Career Ambitions:** Reflect on your conversations about career paths and ambitions. Do both of you feel understood and supported in your professional journeys? Schedule regular check-ins to discuss any changes or challenges.

3. **Quality Over Quantity:** While work demands may sometimes limit the time available together, how can you make the most of the moments you have? Consider ways to infuse quality into the time spent with your partner, ensuring a meaningful connection.

_____

_____

_____

_____

_____

CHAPTER 9

Mental Health Issues

Understanding, Supporting, Healing Together

In the warmth of their living room, sunlight streamed through the curtains, creating golden patterns on the floor. But for Jeremy, the world outside felt endlessly cloudy, a persistent gray that loomed over him.

Emma watched him from her seat, her heart weighed down with concern. The vibrant Jeremy she cherished, who recounted childhood memories with happiness or delved deep into book discussions, seemed distant. This introspective version of him, engrossed in his own world, was a version Emma tried to comprehend. His behavior had shifted: the countless moments he spent lost in thought, a diminishing passion for things they loved together, and a constant weariness that wasn't just physical.

On a tranquil evening, the ambient sounds of nature serving as their backdrop, Emma walked over with two warm cups of coffee. Choosing her words with care, she began, "Jer-

emy, there's a distance in you. It's not just the quiet, it's the depth of it. Can we talk about what's going on?"

Meeting her gaze, Jeremy's eyes welled up. "It feels like I'm drowning, Em. Every day feels like a battle to stay afloat. Everything seems so...colorless."

Drawing a deep breath, Emma softly responded, "We'll get through this." She drew him close, her embrace a cocoon of reassurance. "We'll seek the help we need, understand this together, and face it side by side."

Hesitatingly, Jeremy replied, "I don't even know where to start, Em."

With the familiar strength that had always grounded them, Emma held him tighter. "I might not have all the answers, but I'm here, by your side. We have each other and love to guide us. We can do this. Together."

Their path forward was not clear-cut, but they had made a crucial beginning: recognizing the insidious shadow of mental health challenges. With empathy, patience, and the support of a mental health professional, they were determined to rediscover their shared happiness and restore the vibrant hues to their life.

Setting the Stage

Mental health is an often-overlooked thread in marital bonds that can deeply impact its design. While love, trust, and understanding are the pillars of a successful marriage, mental health issues can subtly introduce complexities that may go unnoticed until they have woven their patterns deep into the relationship. As one partner grapples with their internal struggles, the ripples are felt throughout the union, sometimes causing dissonance in a previously harmonious relationship.

Imagine a bond where both partners once reveled in shared laughter, joys, and dreams. However, with the onset of mental health challenges, the dynamics shift. Moments of clarity can be overshadowed by periods of emotional withdrawal, unpredictability, or profound sadness. The partner not experiencing these challenges may oscillate between roles of a caregiver, confidante, and, at times, a lonely observer, yearning to return their beloved's familiar essence.

In this chapter, we journey into how mental health can influence the ebb and flow of marital dynamics. While the challenges may seem daunting, they offer growth opportunities, deeper understanding, and a more profound connection. Navigating the unpredictable seas of mental health within marriage requires patience, resilience, and an untiring commitment to learning.

As we explore further, we will also highlight the importance of seeking timely help for the affected individual and the relationship. Because even amidst the trials of mental health issues, there lies the potential for a bond that emerges stronger, more compassionate, and infinitely more understanding.

Let's lay the foundation by looking at the research on this.

In-Depth Research Dive

Depression, a widespread mental health issue, can introduce unique challenges to a marital relationship. According to Whisman (2001), married individuals with depressive symptoms are more likely to report marital dissatisfaction than those without. The ripple effect of depression, characterized by feelings of hopelessness, fatigue, and irritability, can undermine a couple's ability to connect emotionally and resolve conflicts. This emotional disconnection can lead to misunderstandings and reinforce negative interaction patterns, increasing the risk of marital discord.

Anxiety disorders, encompassing generalized anxiety disorder, panic disorder, and social anxiety disorder, can similarly pose challenges in marital dynamics. Blandon, Calkins, Keane, and O'Brien (2008) explored the relationship between marital functioning and anxiety disorders and discovered that heightened marital stress often coexists with elevated anxiety symptoms. The constant state of worry and the physical symptoms accompanying anxiety, such as tremors, rapid heartbeat, or breathlessness, can inhibit the formation of a safe emotional space for both partners. In such cases, the partner without an anxiety disorder might feel on edge, unsure of how to support the affected partner effectively.

While depression and anxiety disorders are prevalent, personality disorders also play a significant role in marital dynamics. South, Turkheimer, and Oltmanns (2008) discussed the impact of personality disorders, such as borderline and antisocial personality disorders, on marriages. These disorders often manifest as erratic behaviors, impulsivity, and difficulty maintaining stable relationships. Their study found that these personality disorders in one or both partners are associated with lower marital satisfaction and stability, partly because of the difficulties in understanding and navigating the unpredictable nature of such conditions.

The challenges of obsessive-compulsive disorder (OCD) in marital relationships should not be overlooked. Abramowitz, Baucom, Boeding, and Wheaton (2013) delved into the effects of OCD symptoms on marital satisfaction. Their findings indicated that partners of individuals with OCD often find themselves trapped in the rituals and compulsions of the affected partner, leading to frustration and relationship strain. The relentless need for reassurance and repetitive behaviors can become a significant stressor, eroding the couple's sense of intimacy and shared experiences.

Bipolar disorder, with its distinct episodes of mania and depression, can complicate marital dynamics. According to Lam, Donaldson, Brown, and Malliaris (2005), the unpredictable shifts in mood, energy, and activity levels associated with bipolar disorder can introduce significant challenges to relationships. Partners may find it challenging to discern whether certain behaviors or reactions are symptomatic of the illness or genuine reflections of their partner's feelings. This uncertainty can lead to heightened tensions and frequent misunderstandings, often escalating conflicts in marital settings.

Schizophrenia, although less prevalent than other mental health disorders, can profoundly impact marital relationships. Tarrier and Wykes (2004) explored how the positive symptoms of schizophrenia, such as hallucinations and delusions, and the negative symptoms, like social withdrawal and lack of emotion, affect partners and marriages. Often, the partner without schizophrenia can feel overwhelmed by the effort required to support their spouse, leading to isolation and loneliness. The unpredictable nature of schizophrenia and potential disruptions in daily life can add significant strain, with partners often feeling they are navigating the challenges alone.

Post-Traumatic Stress Disorder (PTSD) stemming from traumatic events can also deeply affect marital stability. Monson, Taft, and Fredman (2009) highlighted couples' challenges when one partner has PTSD. Symptoms like re-experiencing traumatic events, increased arousal, and avoidance behaviors can create barriers to emotional intimacy. The study found that PTSD affects the diagnosed individual and extends its reach to partners, who often report feeling emotionally distant or walking on eggshells around the affected spouse. The secondary trauma experienced by the partner can lead to mental health challenges, compounding the strains on the marriage.

Attention-Deficit/Hyperactivity Disorder (ADHD) in adults, though often associated with children, plays a substantial role in marital dynamics. According to Wymbs et al. (2008), marriages where one partner has ADHD often experience higher levels of dysfunction. The core symptoms of ADHD, including impulsivity, inattention, and hyperactivity, can manifest as forgetfulness, difficulty completing tasks, and frequent conversation interruptions. The unaffected partner can misinterpret such behaviors as consideration or lack of interest, leading to frustration and dissatisfaction in the marriage.

Reflections and Insights

Over the course of my 25-year marriage, I've ascended the ranks in various organizations. Parallel to my professional journey has been a deepening comprehension of mental health and its intricate facets.

Entering the workforce, I was laden with emotional burdens I barely recognized, my grasp on mental health being primarily informed by witnessing the most severe episodes of my mother's challenges. As I progressed in my career, the indicators of mental distress became more apparent: staff members confronting invisible battles, seats once alive with productivity now eerily silent, and the devastating reality of some colleagues choosing to end their pain permanently.

As the gravity of these situations dawned on the corporate world, interventions were initiated. Employee Assistance Programs (EAPs) emerged, offering more than just a helpline – they became a beacon of hope, a reassuring voice on the other end of the line. I transitioned from rudimentary awareness to recognizing the imperative for comprehensive mental health strategies within the corporate environment.

Yet, academia had its share of shadows. In college, I was deeply shaken by the news of a fellow student taking their life over an imperfect grade. These devastating events often remained behind a curtain of silence, with a heavier focus on the aftermath rather than addressing the underlying triggers. This silence wasn't confined to educational institutions. Relocating my family to a Dallas suburb, its unsettling proximity to an area colloquially dubbed "Suicide High," starkly underscored the breadth and depth of the mental health crisis.

But it was in my capacity as a business leader that my perspective truly transformed. Identifying an employee grappling with mental health challenges, and understanding its potential ramifications on the business, allowed me to draw parallels between my personal encounters and the broader workplace context. It fostered in me a profound empathy for those in turmoil and heightened my awareness of its implications for organizational well-being.

Recognizing the humanity behind each employee number, each student ID, was not just an exercise in empathy but also a crucial understanding for effective leadership. After all, business and academia don't operate in vacuums; they're powered by individuals, each with their own challenges and stories.

The Unseen Baggage: Emotional Legacies in Relationships

Every relationship begins with a blending of sweet and painful histories. Just as we carry our moments of joy and achievements, we also lug with us the shadows of past experiences and events that shaped our beliefs, attitudes, fears, and hopes. This emotional baggage can range from past heartbreaks to the complexities of familial relations.

Growing up in the shadow of my mother's mental health challenges was not merely about understanding her battles but navigating my experiences, feelings, and emotions alongside hers. Witnessing her fight was not like watching from the sidelines; it felt like I was in the arena with her, facing every high and low, every moment of clarity and confusion. The hospital visits, the whispered conversations in hushed tones, and the evident strain it brought upon our family life became as much a part of my childhood as any other memory.

Such early exposure to mental health struggles might confuse a young mind. As children, we are often more perceptive than adults give us credit for. While I could not always comprehend the depth of her condition, the environment it created – the unpredictability of her moods, the undercurrents of tension at home, the shifts from laughter to tears – left an indelible mark on me.

During these tumultuous experiences, there existed a stark contradiction that puzzled me for years: my mother's vibrant, engaging persona. She was a beacon of love and guidance to the outside world and, indeed, to most of our family. When she sang, her voice was the embodiment of pure emotion, resonating with all who heard it. As a dedicated attendee at numerous funerals, she showed an unwavering commitment to be there for others during their grief.

As the family historian, her stories bridged generations, weaving a tapestry of our shared past. Everyone remembered her laugh – it was infectious, genuine, and one of the most reassuring sounds of my childhood. Her embraces were havens of comfort, where one felt seen and cherished. It was a jarring juxtaposition: this effervescent, larger-than-life figure and the mental health challenges she silently grappled with. As a child, reconciling these two facets was difficult. It often led to moments of deep reflection, trying to make sense of the duality of her nature. How could someone so full of life, so deeply rooted in the heart of our family, also wrestle with such profound internal struggles?

With these memories came many apprehensions that carried forward into my adult life. The love and concern I felt for my mother coexisted with a gnawing fear about the nature of relationships. Was every relationship doomed to have undercurrents of tension? Despite my best intentions, would I inadvertently carry some of these patterns into my marriage?

This was not about blame but an earnest reflection. The unpredictable nature of my mother's condition made me wonder about our roles in our relationships. How much of our past experiences do we, knowingly or unknowingly, superimpose on our present? And, more importantly, how do these imprints affect our relationships?

Navigating these questions is not about finding definitive answers but recognizing the weight of the past, we bring into our relationships. Acknowledging them, we take the first step toward understanding, healing, and building deeper, more aware connections.

From Desolation to Discovery: A Journey through Hidden Battles

Before Bonita graced my life, I was wading through a dense fog of despair. Three years before our paths crossed, I had been dismissed from college due to poor grades, marking the beginning of a downward spiral. Returning to Dallas, I felt the world's weight was on my shoulders. I thought I had let down everyone – my family, friends, and educators. But beyond that heavy weight was the silent struggle I faced. No one knew the backstory, the quiet hunger and challenges that pulled me down.

No one knows the person behind the mask until the stage lights dim and the crowd's applause fades into silence. For me, a parallel world of struggles and unspoken pains existed beneath the achievements and the limelight.

"Hey, aren't you T-Bone?" I would occasionally hear it on the streets of Dallas. It was a name that echoed back to my glory days where I set stadiums ablaze with my performances as the acclaimed drum major. The sheer energy, the magnetic pull I had on the crowds, the admiration – it was electric. And it was not just the field. Turning on the TV, you would hear a catchy jingle from the Dallas County Community College commercial, a rhythmic "Go to School, Don't Be a Fool, Get an Education!" And there I was, pivoting from the piano to face the audience, declaring with pride, "You want to know my major? Electrical Engineering!"

Yet, the stark juxtaposition of my past to my present reality was heart-wrenching. Here I was, fresh from the acclaim of high school, from being the face of campaigns and winning a flurry of scholarships, now clad in a construction worker's attire. The sun's heat, the grueling ten-hour shifts, the sweat trailing down my spine – it was a world apart from the piano keys and the drum major's baton. Boarding the bus after those endless shifts, I would catch glimpses of women, their eyes heavy with pity and judgment, as if silently saying, "I could never date a man like you."

One evening, as I leaned into the window in my bus seat, lost in a sea of thoughts, a gentle voice broke my trance. An elderly lady with lines of wisdom etched on her face leaned in, "You're T-Bone, aren't you?" she asked, her eyes sparkling with recognition. "You were so good on that football field. I loved the band. You used to dance and make everyone's day."

I managed a tired smile, nodding. "Yes, ma'am, I was." I said, recalling my time as a four-year drummajor at my high school.

Her face brightened, recognition dawning. "I'm Fred's mother."

A torrent of memories rushed in. Fred's name, his legacy, echoed in my mind. Fred Baker, the "Touchdown Maker," was the undeniable heartbeat of our high school football team. Every game day, the power trinity of our school emerged: me as the head drum major, Fred electrifying the field as the star running back, and Tim leading the vibrant color guard. We were the titans of our time, leaders in our domains, the pride of our school.

But Fred's name carried more than high school memories and electrifying touchdowns. It brought the weight of a tragic past. Fred was murdered my sophomore year, the casualty of a bullet that silenced the roars of those that anticipated cheering for him the next school year. However, that summer bullet replaced that aspiration with cries of anguish. As those memories surged back, my vision blurred, tears threatening to spill.

Fred's mother, despite the mountains of grief she carried, reached out to comfort me. "It's alright, baby. Fred loved you," she whispered, her voice warm and comforting. It astounded me. Here was a woman who had lost her son, yet she was offering comfort to someone who, in comparison, had lost so much less.

Our conversation on the bus ride reopened old wounds, especially the tragic loss of my 16-year-old cousin Tyrone of a drug-related murder and my friend Keith during my sophomore year. Keith's had been killed at a gameroom just a year before that bus ride, and I was still reeling from the deaths of my first cousins Debra, Carl, Roderick, and Walter.

The mention of Fred's name triggered those other memories. She prepared to leave the bus and whispered, "You are still T-Bone. Your struggles don't define you. We all face battles. God bless you, son."

Meeting Fred's mother again underscored life's complexities of joy, tragedy, and resilience. However, these hopeful moments were islands in a sea of my internal struggles.

Many saw my college dismissal as the start of my decline. Returning to Dallas, I felt the weight of 'failure' and 'disappointment' at every turn. That was a painful blow, certainly, that sent me reeling back to Dallas burdened with the stinging labels of 'failure' and 'disappointment.' Every step I took felt heavy, every gaze I met seemed judgmental, and every reflection in the mirror was a harsh reminder of unmet potential.

But the truth was, this period of academic struggle was only the tip of the iceberg. Beneath were deeper traumas. The world saw a stumbling student, unaware of the young man battling past shadows.

Haunted by the tragic losses, even as I succeeded in high school, the streets of our youth roared cautionary tales. Balancing public celebrations with private grief was exhausting.

It wasn't just about personal losses or academic setbacks. It was the challenge of navigating societal perceptions and confronting emotional baggage from the past.

In that silence, I would often remind myself – I was T-Bone. And if there was anything that name stood for, it was resilience, passion, and the will to rise, no matter the odds.

The people who once claimed to be my friends and college peers did not return my calls. A number of past relationships crumbled, replaced by "looks of disappointment" I perceived. Home, a place of comfort and warmth, was no longer available.

My mother, once my rock, had married an abusive man and found my presence inconvenient. This relegated me to the uncomfortable corners of my aunts' rat and roach-infested homes. (One aunt would not even allow me to eat what she bought her sons, yet after I found my first job, she harassed me for payment because I had slept on her floor.) The isolation was so profound that I pulled away from every support system I once had – from my alma mater, where I had helped students, to my spiritual haven, the church.

During Desert Storm, my steadfast ally, my sister, was deployed. Upon her return, she invited me to a church revival, a moment that would pivot the course of my life. This revival showcased five pastors from the revered Bishop College, each delivering profound messages.

One pastor's sermon on "The Order of Breaking Bread" struck a chord within me. His poignant words, "God Takes You, He Blesses You, He Breaks You, and He Uses You," became an anchor during turbulent times. As the weight of those words settled, I was overcome with emotion. It was in this raw moment that my sister glimpsed the true extent of my despair, previously unaware of the dark thoughts that plagued me.

After the service, my sister, seeing through my façade, asked about my well-being.

"What's going on with you?" she asked, her voice gentle but insistent. Her question was not just about my current situation; it was an appeal to unlock years of silent anguish.

Taking a deep breath, I began, "Everything. I am homeless. You know they (my aunts) have me sleeping on the floor. Now that I have a job, they keep calling me asking for more money. I cannot even eat their food..." I continued.

Her eyes, now glistening with tears and anger, met mine with a deep understanding I had not seen in anyone for a long time. "I didn't know," she whispered.

Moved by my plight, my sister said, 'Stay with me.' Her offer was not just about a place to live; it was an embrace of understanding and assurance that I wasn't alone.

My sister's friends welcomed me, contrasting our mother's decisions shaped by her battles. My sister became more than family; she was my beacon during my darkest moments.

From Shadows to Light: Preparing for Commitment

The hues of previous experiences color every chapter of life. I was no exception. As I entered the most intimate relationship of my life, marrying Bonita, the specters of my past followed me, painting a backdrop of hesitations, anxieties, and shadows. But these were not the outcomes of diagnosed mental illnesses; they were the scars and stories of years lived in the turbulent shadow of my mother's very real battle with mental health.

When one grows up in a household marred by mental illness, it becomes nearly impossible not to question one's mental stability. Questions like, "Am I okay?" or "Will I follow the same path?" become an intrinsic part of one's self-dialogue. This is not a reflection of self-doubt but rather an inevitable introspection borne from witnessing the struggles of a loved one.

My experiences before Bonita were ones of turbulence. Despite my sister's valiant attempts to shield and support me, the weight of past baggage bore down heavily on my psyche. This was not just emotional luggage; it was a repository of experiences, fears, and anxieties that had shaped my world view. It was not a clinically diagnosed mental illness but the mental residue of years spent navigating the complexities of a family dynamic that had been warped by one.

Entering a relationship, especially one as profound as marriage, meant introducing Bonita to this maze of my past. It was not about seeking sympathy but ensuring she understood the intricate web of experiences that shaped me. I felt responsible for illuminating these corners, providing our foundation was of understanding, trust, and shared perspective.

As I delved into these discussions, what became evident was the depth of Bonita's empathy. She did not just listen; she sought to understand, placing herself in the shoes of a young man trying to find his footing amidst familial chaos. Our dialogues about my mother's battles, her diagnosis, and the toll it took on our family became essential landmarks in our journey together. It underscored the importance of mental health awareness as a societal concern and an intimate facet of our shared life.

Mental health is a spectrum, and while I may not have been on the severe end of it, I carried the experiences and nuances of someone who had seen its effects up close. With Bonita's unwavering support, I realized that our shared journey was not just about understanding each other but also about learning from and supporting one another through our unique struggles.

Drawing the Line

In sharing my story, I aim to distinguish between hardships and clinically diagnosed mental illness. They may evoke similar emotional responses but stem from different origins and demand distinct forms of support.

Life's Hardships vs. Mental Illness: The Key Differences

- **Duration and Persistence:** One of the defining differences between the ups and downs we face in life and a diagnosed mental illness is the duration and persistence of symptoms. While everyone might feel sad, overwhelmed, or anxious occasionally, those with a mental illness often experience these feelings intensely, for extended periods, and sometimes without apparent reason.

- **Severity of Symptoms:** Life's challenges can bring about stress, sadness, or anxiety. However, in cases of mental illness, the symptoms are often more severe. For instance, while grief or a break-up might cause temporary depressive feelings, clinical depression can lead to profound feelings of worthlessness, significant weight changes, prolonged sleep disturbances, or even thoughts of suicide.

- **Impairment in Daily Life:** Mental illnesses tend to result in notable impairments in daily life. This could manifest in the inability to perform everyday tasks, hold a job, maintain relationships, or care for oneself. On the other hand, while life's struggles can be challenging, they usually do not hinder a person's ability to function in the long run.

- **Response to Support and Time:** Generally, the natural ebbs and flows of life, with time and supportive environments, see a reduction in intensity. The pain of a loss or the stress of a job change will lessen as one adapts or as time passes. On the contrary, mental illnesses often require more structured interventions, such as therapy or medication, and might not necessarily "improve" with time alone.

- Physiological Causes: While life challenges and mental illnesses can have biological implications, conditions like bipolar disorder, schizophrenia, or major depressive disorder often have underlying physiological factors. This could be an imbalance in brain chemistry, genetic factors, or other biological triggers. In contrast, the hardships of life, like a job loss or a relationship breakdown, are typically external situational triggers.

Understanding these distinctions is paramount, especially in relationships. The way one supports a partner dealing with the grief of losing a parent versus a partner grappling with bipolar disorder will necessarily differ. Both require empathy, understanding, and love, but the latter also requires a structured, informed approach that may involve professionals, sustained treatments, and ongoing education.

In highlighting my journey, my goal is to shed light on these differences and emphasize the importance of clear communication and understanding, especially in romantic partnerships. Recognizing the difference between a bad day and a depressive episode or understanding the chasm between feeling stressed and having an anxiety disorder can be pivotal in nurturing relationships that flourish amidst challenges. When we equip ourselves with knowledge and understanding, we move from merely sympathizing to deeply empathizing, ensuring that our relationships are not just about navigating storms together but also about turning challenges into opportunities for deeper connection and growth.

Strategies for Improvement

The intricate dance of marriage becomes particularly complex when navigating the shadows of mental health challenges. Whether it's anxiety, depression, or any other condition, these invisible weights can add complexity to the already delicate equilibrium of a marital bond. The emotional and behavioral shifts associated with mental health can create cracks of misunderstanding, even in the strongest unions. For couples grappling with such challenges, acknowledging the impact of these conditions is the first step toward resilience. It's crucial to foster an environment of compassion, patience, and continuous learning. Seeking professional guidance, embracing therapeutic interventions, and ensuring open lines of communication can be instrumental in maintaining stability. When couples unite to face the specter of mental health issues, they fortify their bond and create a sanctuary of understanding and support within their marriage.

Couples can find a way forward together with the right strategies and understanding. Based on rigorous academic exploration, here are some seminal strategies that couples can embrace to navigate the maze of mental health challenges in marriage:

- **Early Recognition & Intervention:** Identifying early signs of mental health challenges and seeking timely intervention can prevent escalation and strain on the relationship (Kessler, Chiu, Demler, & Walters, 2005).

- **Continuous Education:** Invest time in understanding each other's mental health conditions. This fosters empathy and equips both partners to handle challenges better (Whisman, 2007).

- **Joint Counseling:** Engaging in couple's therapy can provide tools and strategies to navigate the relationship dynamics impacted by mental health concerns (Bodenmann, Plancherel, Beach, Widmer, & Gabriel, 2008).

- **Develop Coping Mechanisms:** Jointly identifying and practicing healthy coping strategies can reduce stress and promote understanding (Amato & Rogers, 1997).

- **Promote Individual Well-being:** Encourage each other to seek individual therapy or support groups, ensuring personal well-being, which can subsequently strengthen the marital bond (Coyne, Thompson, & Palmer, 2002).

- **Foster Open Dialogue:** Create a safe space for open conversations about feelings, concerns, and fears related to mental health (Beach & O'Leary, 1993).

- **Establish Support Networks:** Surround yourself with supportive friends and family who understand and respect a marriage's mental health management journey (Proulx, Helms, & Buehler, 2007).

Reflective Prompts

Finally, here are three questions to ask yourself to deal with mental health challenges in your marriage:

1. **Understanding and Patience:** Reflect on understanding your partner's mental health challenges. Are there aspects you find difficult to grasp? Consider seeking resources or counseling to deepen your comprehension and empathy.

2. **Open Conversations:** How frequently do you discuss mental well-being in your relationship? Creating a safe space for regular check-ins can help both partners feel supported and understood.

3. **Seeking Help Together:** Consider the benefits of attending therapy or counseling together. Collaborative healing can strengthen the bond and mutual understanding even if only one partner faces a mental health challenge.

_____

_____

_____

_____

_____

_____

CHAPTER 10

Lack of Effort

Reigniting Passion, Sustaining Love

As the evening sky deepened to an illuminated blue, the sounds of a once lively home had turned to whispers. Once bustling with shared cooking experiments, the kitchen saw hurried microwave dinners. Once filled with laughter and movie nights, the house had become two separate islands of solitude: Tameka was engrossed in catching up on Facebook in the bedroom, and Dennis was lost in his endless practicing of the guitar in the basement.

The effortless ease they once enjoyed had, over time, morphed into routine apathy. Small gestures of love – a surprise note, a spontaneous hug, or even just a simple shared joke – had dwindled.

One Sunday morning, Tameka, looking through their old photo albums, paused at a picture from their early dating days – a cruise excursion where they had laughed through the rain and mud. The contrast was stark and heart-wrenching.

She placed the album in front of Dennis. "Look at us," she said, her voice laced with nostalgia and hurt. "What happened?"

Dennis sighed deeply, recognizing the distance they had unknowingly allowed to creep in. "We stopped trying," he admitted, tracing the edges of a photo with his finger.

"We've become complacent," Tameka whispered, "thinking love will sustain itself without nurturing."

The realization hung heavy between them. But in that moment of mutual acknowledgment, a spark of their former connection ignited. Determined not to let their bond dissolve into indifference, they pledged to reinvest in their relationship, reminding themselves that love, like any other precious thing, requires regular care and effort to flourish truly.

Setting the Stage

At the heart of every blossoming relationship is an underlying current of effort, propelling it forward and ensuring its vitality. In its very essence, marriage is not a passive undertaking but rather a proactive commitment. Both partners unite, pledging to work, nurturing the bond, and fostering growth. However, as days turn to years and life's other demands jostle for attention, the foundation of effort that once seemed so strong can start to wane.

Envision a once-loved and cared-for garden bursting with vibrant blooms. Without consistent effort, the flowers begin to wilt, the ground becomes parched, and what was once a sanctuary of beauty reflects neglect. Similarly, a marriage without continued effort begins to show signs of weariness. The sweet nothings, the spontaneous acts of love, and the quality time shared – when taken for granted – can lead the relationship into a silent dormancy.

This chapter delves into the often-understated importance of sustained effort in marital dynamics. The nuances of everyday life, the complacency that sets in with familiarity, and the erroneous belief that love alone is sufficient can all contribute to this lapse. However, the magic of marriage is that, with intent and action, couples can reignite that initial spark, reminding themselves and each other why they chose this shared journey.

As we journey through these pages, we will also emphasize the significance of conscious engagement and how couples can reintroduce effort into their relationship. Because in love and togetherness, effort is not just a choice; it is a continuous pledge to prioritize the bond over everything else.

To set the stage, let's first dive into the research concerning this topic.

In-Depth Research Dive

Boredom in relationships has been studied for its detrimental impact on marital satisfaction. According to Tsapelas, Aron, and Orbuch (2009), when couples experience prolonged periods of boredom, they are more likely to report decreased satisfaction over time. The study emphasized that couples actively seeking shared novel experiences are less likely to suffer from this decline in relationship quality. Engaging in new activities can serve as a countermeasure against the feelings of monotony and stagnation that often accompany diminished effort in the relationship.

Compromised communication stands as another significant consequence of decreased effort in marriages. Neff and Karney (2004) found that couples not prioritizing open and constructive communication tend to experience increased stress and conflict. Their study revealed that when couples allow external stressors to dictate the communication patterns within the relationship, it results in diminished resilience against marital challenges. Regular, quality communication is a buffer, safeguarding the relationship against external pressures.

Changing priorities, particularly when not communicated, can create rifts in marriages. Stanley, Rhoades, and Whitton (2010) explored "sliding versus deciding," where couples either passively slide into major relationship transitions or actively decide and plan them together. The study found that couples who regularly slide into major changes without mutual discussions are more likely to face relationship dissatisfaction and instability. This underscores the importance of mutual effort in ensuring both partners are aligned in their relationship goals and aspirations.

The decline of physical intimacy due to a lack of effort has also been a focal point of marital research. According to Mark, Laurenceau, and Gonzaga (2018), couples who experience prolonged periods without physical intimacy report higher levels of distress, reduced relationship satisfaction, and decreased feelings of closeness. Physical intimacy serves not only as a foundation of marital connection but also as a barometer for the overall health and vitality of the relationship. Thus, its decline often signifies deeper unresolved issues and unmet needs within the partnership.

Financial strain is another substantial factor magnified by a lack of effort in marital relationships. According to Dew, Britt, and Huston (2012), economic difficulties can amplify existing relationship problems, especially when couples are not actively collaborating to address financial challenges. Their study identified that couples who displayed a combined lack of effort in managing their finances reported more frequent conflicts, mistrust, and lower marital satisfaction. In contrast, couples who approached their economic challenges as a team were better equipped to weather financial storms and maintained higher levels of relationship satisfaction.

Children and parenting also introduce new dynamics to the marital relationship, and decreasing effort can intensify associated challenges. According to Kluwer and Johnson (2007), when partners fail to communicate effectively about parenting responsibilities and philosophies, it often increases stress and resentment. Their research emphasized the importance of active co-parenting strategies and collaboration. The findings highlighted that when one partner perceives a lack of effort from the other in parenting roles, it can lead to an overall decline in marital satisfaction and, in extreme cases, even the contemplation of separation.

The roles of external relationships, such as friendships and familial bonds, play a pivotal role in how couples perceive effort within their marriage. According to Julien, Chartrand, and Bégin (1999), feelings of jealousy, neglect, and competition can emerge when partners perceive that their spouse is putting more effort into external relationships than the marital bond. The study reinforced that maintaining a balance in external relationships and ensuring that the marriage relationship remains a priority is crucial for sustaining marital health.

Lastly, personal growth and individual aspirations can be overlooked when there is a decrease in mutual effort. Lauer, Lauer, and Kerr (1990) explored the importance of supporting each other's personal growth within marriage. They found that when partners felt unsupported in their aspirations, they reported higher feelings of entrapment and decreased marital satisfaction. Ensuring both partners actively understand and support each other's goals and dreams remains integral to fostering a lasting bond and overall relationship contentment.

Reflections and Insights

In the corporate world, there's a subtle phenomenon known as "quiet quitting." On the surface, individuals seem engaged, maintaining their roles and responsibilities. But beneath that facade, there's a significant drop in passion, dedication, and efficiency. As a seasoned executive who has spearheaded multiple organizations, I've developed a keen eye for spotting the difference between someone genuinely committed and another merely going through the motions.

I recall a leader directly reporting to me grappling with a desire to leave the company. Rather than confronting this wish outright, he chose a passive route, intentionally under-performing in hopes the organization would eventually let him go. This tactic is not unlike certain dynamics in relationships. Sometimes, individuals find themselves in unfulfilling partnerships. But instead of mustering the courage to address the issues or end the relationship, they subtly pull away, hoping their partner will take the initiative to end things. This lack of effort, whether in business or relationships, stems from a fear of confrontation, a hope to avoid blame or the comfort of familiarity, even if it's not truly fulfilling.

Navigating Relationship Effort Over Time

It's not like we've had a smooth ride the whole way. Growing up, neither of us had shining examples of what top-tier effort in a relationship looked like. This meant we had our fair share of missteps, learning as we went. Bonita and I were wary of letting our connection slip due to a lack of effort, especially as time passed.

With each passing year in a relationship, there's a risk that the enthusiasm fades and the drive to try new things diminishes. The spark at the start doesn't necessarily feel the same at years 5, 10, 15, or, in our case, 25. I've realized that effort isn't just about the big gestures at home – it's also about how we show up in public.

For instance, do you still put in the same effort when you're out with your partner? It's not enough to try when it's the two of you at dinner. If she loves attending shows, shopping, or church, does she also feel your support and presence in those moments? Considering how much of our lives are taken up by work, making our partners feel valued in every setting becomes even more crucial.

To the outside world, it might seem like I'm nailing this aspect, often being the only guy at many social events. But it's not about micromanaging or keeping a score. Being there can mean the world if an event is intended for both partners. It's about backing up those you care about. The same goes the other way too. If there's something I'm passionate about, the level of my wife's engagement shows her commitment to us. It's a two-way street. The essence of effort extends beyond the comfort of our homes and into every facet of our shared lives.

Bonita and I always keep things fun and fresh between us. We love seeking new adventures to spice up our days, moving away from the same old routine.

We'd get caught up in their school events and games when our kids were younger. But now that they're older and have their lives, we've been finding new things to enjoy together. We might hit up a casino, watch a show in Vegas, travel to a new place, or try a new dish at a local eatery or home. These shared moments have kept us close.

But what's important is ensuring we truly listen to each other, not getting too wrapped up in our phones or to-do lists. Life can be a whirlwind, especially as we adjust to things now that our kids are all grown up. However, by always finding new ways to connect and ensuring we focus on each other, we've kept our relationship strong.

All of this has shown us that if you want a relationship to last, you've got to put in the effort. Any couple can keep things fresh and exciting by talking openly, trying new things together, and always looking for ways to grow.

Poor Communications

Effective communication is the cornerstone of a resilient relationship. Without it, misunderstandings can escalate into conflicts, creating a rift between partners. When individuals fail to express themselves authentically and transparently, a sense of distance can emerge, leading one or both parties to disengage from making genuine efforts in the relationship. For instance, if someone perceives their partner is not truly listening or understanding them, they may retreat, reducing their input and commitment.

Poor communication can breed misconceptions, disagreements, and overall discontentment, potentially elevating the risk of separation. However, by identifying and addressing communication barriers, couples can enhance their understanding of one another, reinforcing their bond. By refining their communication strategies, partners mitigate conflicts and lay the foundation for a deeper, more harmonious connection.

Bonita and I have prioritized cultivating open and honest communication to avoid falling into this trap. We recognize that misunderstandings and conflicts are inevitable. Still, by actively working on our communication skills, we have addressed these challenges head-on and prevented them from causing a rift in our relationship.

One thing we do is reserve dinner time every day to talk openly while having dinner. We start with a simple question like "How was your day?" This question is open-ended so that we can talk about anything. When we have these talks, we share what is on our minds and how we feel. This gives us a safe place to listen and understand each other. Doing this has kept us close and aware of the other partner's needs. It has stopped small misunderstandings from taking the form of big problems.

Also, actively listening isn't just a courtesy – it's a necessity in nurturing relationships. Admittedly, one challenge I continually grapple with is not diving into conversations with my preconceptions or prematurely offering solutions, especially before Bonita has had the chance to share her thoughts fully.

With over two decades as a leader in the corporate world, my voice often carries weight, guiding many discussions. While invaluable at work, this influential role doesn't always translate seamlessly to home dynamics. There's a marked difference between leading a team at the office and being an equal partner at home. The lines can blur, but it's essential to delineate the two.

My prolonged hours at work shape my professional identity and can inadvertently mold my personal one. This intertwining can sometimes make work the dominant part of my identity. In our relationship, I need to set aside that corporate persona and assume what I see as a humbler, service-oriented role at home.

I've observed parallels in how my children interact with Bonita and me. While they frequently chat with her about their day or life's nuances, their calls to me are typically more problem-centered. It's akin to how my team might approach me – a testament to respect, no doubt, but it also highlights a challenge. I'm often seen as the "problem solver," which, while flattering, can sometimes make it hard to switch off that instinct.

If left unchecked, this leadership dynamic at work can inadvertently create barriers at home. My deliberate decision to set aside the "boss" persona is not just about balance but creating a space where Bonita doesn't feel overshadowed. When we converse about our aspirations, concerns, or daily matters, it's paramount that we stand on equal ground, with every word and feeling validated.

Understanding and actively managing this crossover between work and home roles is vital for couples, especially in long-term partnerships. When accustomed to leading or solving problems in the professional sphere, it's easy to diminish the effort needed at home unintentionally. Recognizing these potential pitfalls and consciously adjusting paves the way for both partners to invest genuine effort in fortifying their bond.

Lastly, we show how much we value each other often. This might mean extending birthday celebrations to a whole week instead of just a day or giving gifts at unexpected times, not just on holidays. By focusing on the good things in our relationship, we remind ourselves why we are together and keep our promise to take care of our marriage.

Through these intentional communication practices, Bonita and I have avoided the pitfalls of poor communication and maintained a healthy marriage. As it turns out to be a tried and tested method in my marriage, open and honest dialogue, coupled with active listening and regular expressions of gratitude, has proven to be a powerful combination in fostering a resilient and enduring partnership.

Shifting Priorities

As people evolve and shift over time, what is important to them can change, making them spend less time on their relationships. For instance, someone might get really into their job or other personal hobbies, leaving less energy for their marriage. This can hurt the relationship; the couple might feel like they are drifting apart. To stop this from happening, couples need to team up and make sure their relationship stays important. They should set aside time for each other regularly. The secret tip to a healthy marriage is to cherish and celebrate each other every day.

Bonita and I have navigated the challenge of evolving priorities. As we raised our kids, our roles were distinct. She took on the mantle of a stay-at-home mom, overseeing the household finances and managing our children's schedules. In contrast, I was the traveling father, ensuring our income and making concerted efforts to stay connected with our children's engagements.

When our youngest, Tyler, finished high school, Bonita returned to school and worked. After being married for 20 years, we found ourselves in a situation where we were both focused on our careers and new hobbies. We also understood that our relationship could suffer if we did not prioritize it. So, to prevent this, we deliberately chose to keep our marriage at the center of our lives.

We have managed this by planning trips to spend time together regularly. Even with our ever-so-busy lives, we make one trip every three months to reconnect and have fun. These times have kept us close emotionally and reminded us how important our relationship is, even when things are quite busy.

In the early days of our marriage, Bonita was a consistent presence at my blues performances, whether in nightclubs or churches. Similarly, as Bonita dealt with losing her mother and friends to breast cancer, I stood by her side during her Susan G. Komen 3-Day walks. I cheered her on at different points during the 20-mile-a-day walks and celebrated her accomplishments when she earned her degree to begin her career. This mutual support strengthened our bond and helped us grow as individuals and as a couple.

By having open and honest discussions about what matters most to each of us, we can make informed decisions and strike a balance between our individual needs and the needs of our relationship.

Through these intentional efforts, Bonita and I have successfully dealt with the challenge of shifting priorities and ensured that our marriage remains strong and resilient. We have maintained a healthy and thriving partnership despite life's inevitable changes by being available for each other, supporting each other's personal growth, and communicating our priorities.

Financial Pressure

Financial challenges often cast a long shadow over relationships. The strain of monetary issues affects individual well-being and can erode the foundation of trust and understanding between partners. This strain becomes especially palpable when one perceives themselves shouldering the brunt of these burdens, leading to isolation and resentment.

I grappled with these very emotions in the early stages of our marriage. My aspirations for our family seemed to be constantly hampered by our immediate financial hurdles. Even though we had a plan and had successfully navigated our student loans out of default, the added expenses hindered the pace at which I had hoped we would progress toward our other goals. These persistent worries often left me in deep contemplation, prompting Bonita's concerned queries, "Baby, what's wrong?" To which I would typically mask my anxiety, replying, "Nothing..." But beneath that facade, the weight of living paycheck to paycheck gnawed at me.

In retrospect, my reticence was a disservice to both of us. By not sharing my financial concerns, I inadvertently kept Bonita at arm's length from our shared journey. She remained unaware of the depth of my anxiety, believing it was a mere passing phase rather than a profound concern about our future. As our finances gradually stabilized, it became evident that my reserved approach had inadvertently created a communication gap between us. If I had been candid with Bonita from the outset, she would have grasped that my angst was born from a desire to ensure a brighter future for us much sooner than our circumstances seemed to allow. I was navigating the turbulent financial strain without letting her share the burden. This realization underscored the importance of open communication in facing life's challenges together.

Through open dialogue and collaboration, Bonita and I navigated the financial stresses that often strain marriages. By being proactive in the initial years of our union, we successfully met our financial objectives, which safeguarded our relationship from monetary disagreements in the long run. Sharing our feelings, discussing our concerns, and aligning on economic aspirations prevented monetary challenges from casting shadows on our marital bond.

Lack of Physical Intimacy

Not having enough physical closeness can affect how much effort goes into a marriage. Characterized by hugging, kissing, holding hands, and sexual engagement, physical intimacy acts as an unspoken language of love and connection. A deficiency in intimacy can manifest as feelings of isolation and emotional detachment, potentially undermining the relationship's foundation. Feldman (2012) emphasizes the significance of physical touch, noting that it goes beyond the emotional bond by stimulating the release of oxytocin, a hormone that fosters trust and feelings of love.

The implications of inadequate physical intimacy are multifaceted, reaching beyond a lack of intimacy and emotional connection. When couples experience a dip in sexual satisfaction, it can significantly affect overall happiness and contentment in the relationship. Such dissatisfaction, sometimes a function of emotional distance, is also intertwined with physiological factors.

As individuals age, various biological changes influence the dynamics of physical intimacy within a relationship. Men may face testosterone fluctuations and challenges related to erectile function, while women undergoing menopause might grapple with estrogen levels that affect their sexual comfort and desire. Additionally, common health challenges associated with aging, such as arthritis or cardiovascular complications, can hinder physical closeness.

However, it is essential to note that advancing age does not necessarily correlate with a diminished capacity for physical intimacy. It is pivotal to take a proactive stance, marked by open communication about emerging challenges and a mutual commitment to address them. By emphasizing the importance of physical intimacy, couples can reinforce their communication, foster mutual trust, and strengthen their emotional bond, ensuring the relationship remains resilient and fulfilling.

In any marriage, life tends to throw curveballs, testing the resilience of the bond. For Bonita and me, the challenge arrived in a form we had not anticipated: the intersection of health and intimacy. My broken neck and subsequent paralysis were devastating obstacles we bravely faced together. With grit and determination, I managed to regain my health. But another challenge lingered beneath the surface, often more elusive to tackle – the impact of prolonged nerve medication on our physical intimacy.

The issue was not an inability to be intimate. Instead, it was the delicate dance of navigating when to take my prescription for nerve pain management. While beneficial in alleviating my pain, these medications introduced unforeseen side effects that subtly eroded our intimate moments' spontaneity and natural flow. Aging, coupled with the medications, meant becoming intimately familiar with these drugs' consequences on my body and our relationship.

With her ever-present understanding and patience, Bonita joined me in confronting this new challenge. We communicated, openly discussing the hurdles the medications introduced. This dialogue was not just about finding a solution and redefining our norms. It was a journey of rediscovery, learning new rhythms and patterns that would allow us to maintain our intimate connection without letting external factors hinder it.

Just as women often share the nuances of their menstrual cycles with their partners, I recognized the need to be equally transparent with Bonita about my medication's impact on our intimacy.

Physical intimacy is a complex weave of emotion, biology, and circumstance. For Bonita and me, it meant confronting and adapting to challenges and emerging stronger and closer. The essence lies in understanding that openness and communication, even about the most sensitive topics, are the keys to ensuring that external challenges do not define or diminish the love between two people.

A successful marriage requires the continuous commitment of both partners. Though challenges are inevitable, with dedication and effort, the rewards of an enduring partnership are boundless.

Strategies for Improvement

Marriage thrives on consistent dedication and communication. It's a dance that demands both partners be actively engaged. An untended relationship can wither, making the path back to intimacy and understanding arduous. Every gesture, conversation, and shared moment contributes to the vitality of the union. For couples feeling the strain of inertia, it's a call to recommit, to reignite the flames of effort that once burned brightly. Rediscovering shared interests, setting aside time for each other, and taking proactive steps to address challenges can reenergize the marital journey. By embracing the journey with renewed vigor and dedication, couples can ensure that their marital bond remains resilient and enduring.

Life's evolving challenges and shifting priorities can subtly sow the seeds of emotional disconnection between partners. This gradual distancing, if unchecked, can erode the foundation of trust and mutual understanding upon which a marriage is built. Based on exhaustive academic inquiry, the following are foundational strategies that couples can integrate into their relationship to remain aligned and connected:

- **Prioritize Date Nights:** Regularly setting aside quality time strengthens the emotional bond and keeps the romantic spark alive (Aron, Norman, Aron, & Lewandowski, 2002).

- **Engage in Joint Activities:** Pursuing shared hobbies or goals can foster common interests and mutual growth (Reissman, Aron, & Bergen, 1993).

- **Engage in Individual Growth:** Encouraging personal growth and celebrating each other's achievements can prevent resentment and stagnation (Rusbult, Kumashiro, Kubacka, & Finkel, 2009).

- **Practice Active Listening:** Truly hearing and valuing your partner's perspective can prevent feeling undervalued or overlooked (Weger, Castle, & Emmett, 2010).

- **Seek External Support:** Participate in couples retreats or workshops, which can offer fresh insights and revitalize the connection (Halford, Markman, & Stanley, 2008).

- **Revisit Shared Goals:** Regularly discussing future plans and dreams ensures alignment and a shared vision for the journey ahead (Gager & Sanchez, 2003).

- **Establish Routine Check-ins:** Allocating regular emotional check-ins can help address concerns before they amplify (Stanley, Markman, & Whitton, 2002).

Reflective Prompts

Finally, here are three questions to ask yourself to deal with the lack of effort in your marriage:

1. **Revisiting Relationship Milestones:** Think back to the early days of your relationship when efforts to impress and connect were frequent. How can you reintroduce some of those gestures and actions into your current relationship?

2. **Mutual Appreciation:** Reflect on how you appreciate your partner's efforts and how they do the same for you. Regularly acknowledging and valuing each other's efforts can reignite enthusiasm in the relationship.

3. **Commitment to Growth:** Recognize that relationships, like all living things, require nurturing. Are there aspects of the relationship that have been neglected? Brainstorm ways to recommit to its growth, ensuring both partners are actively involved in its cultivation.

_____

_____

_____

_____

_____

_____

_____

The Beginning of Our Journey Together

As we draw to the close of this profound exploration of the challenges faced in marriage and how to overcome them, we must reflect upon our journey. We delved deep into the reasons marriages fail, each representing a unique challenge that couples worldwide grapple with.

Our journey began with exploring the nuances of communication, emphasizing its fundamental importance in marital relationships. We understood how ineffective communication can sow seeds of misunderstanding, conflicts, and emotional distance. Communication is not just about talking; it is about understanding, active listening, empathy, and, most importantly, creating a safe conversation space.

Infidelity, a painful reality for many couples, was discussed in depth. While it is a significant Infidelity, we came to understand that it often stems from a lack of emotional and physical intimacy. This further helped us identify the importance of maintaining intimacy and connection, which forms the lifeblood of any relationship.

We took a deep dive into the complexities of financial disagreements, understanding how money problems are not merely about numbers but often about differing values, expectations, and perceptions. Growing apart, another significant challenge was addressed, emphasizing the need to evolve together as a couple to invest in shared experiences, goals, and dreams.

The influence of external factors, such as family pressures work, and career demands, was explored, emphasizing the need for setting boundaries and balancing responsibilities. We tackled the sensitive issues of substance abuse and mental health problems, understanding their significant impact on a marriage and the need for professional help, empathy, patience, and support.

And lastly, we addressed the danger of complacency, the lack of effort that slowly erodes the bond of marriage. It was clear that constant effort, understanding, and the willingness to work on the relationship are the pillars that uphold a healthy marriage.

As the author, my primary aim was to highlight the challenges and guide couples toward understanding, reconciliation, and growth. This book was a pledge, a commitment toward improving and strengthening marital bonds. My wife Bonita's support and insights have been instrumental in shaping this journey.

The complexity of marriage is not a drawback but its unique strength. Our challenges allow us to learn, grow, and understand our partners better. Marriage is a beautiful amalgamation of two individuals: their dreams, fears, love, and commitment. This book aimed to respect and celebrate this institution's sanctity, providing couples with the insight to build an ever-lasting bond.

A successful marriage is not about evading conflicts or challenges but addressing them together. By fostering effective communication, maintaining intimacy, understanding, and respecting differences, balancing external pressures, addressing mental health and substance abuse issues, and, most importantly, making a consistent effort, you can build a robust foundation for your marriage.

The F.O.R.E.V.E.R. W.E.D. Workbook for Couples

As this book has shed light on critical issues behind marital challenges, remember it is merely the beginning of your journey to a stronger and more fulfilling marriage. Use this knowledge as a foundation for practical action. I am excited to present the F.O.R.E.V.E.R. W.E.D. Workbook for Couples, designed to translate your insights into real-world solutions.

A distinct companion to this book, the F.O.R.E.V.E.R. W.E.D. model is grounded in Christian teachings and captures vital attributes for marital success: Flexibility, Open communication, Respect, Empathy, Vulnerability, Empowerment, Resilience, Wellness, Emotional Intelligence, and Devotion.

While this book has illuminated these foundational principles, the F.O.R.E.V.E.R. W.E.D. workbook delves even deeper, bridging the teachings with a biblical perspective through joint activities and probing questions, couples are facilitated in understanding each other better and aligning their relationship with Christian values and tenets.

The workbook is specifically designed for a range of couples:

- **Pre-Marital Preparation.** For couples seeking a spiritual foundation without undergoing traditional pre-marital counseling.

- **Intimate Conversation Guidance.** For those navigating the complexities of deeper life discussions within the relationship, ensuring that these dialogues resonate with spiritual depth.

- **Church Group Engagement.** Suitable for groups looking for resources that encourage profound reflection and spiritual growth in love and commitment.

With the F.O.R.E.V.E.R. W.E.D. workbook, couples are not merely absorbing information but also actively weaving these principles and biblical teachings into the fabric of their relationship, ensuring a strong, spiritually rooted, and resilient bond. Let this book's conclusion not signal the end but rather a stepping stone to deeper marital exploration with the F.O.R.E.V.E.R. W.E.D. workbook.

True marital fulfillment is not spontaneous – it is constructed. It demands commitment, tools, and consistent effort from both partners. Allow the workbook to guide you on this path toward lasting marital harmony.

In closing, may the lessons, insights, and love from these pages be your compass in the beautiful journey of marriage. Cheers to a lifetime of wedded bliss!

Warmly,
Dr. Cedric Alford

References

Abramowitz, J. S., Baucom, D. H., Boeding, S., & Wheaton, M. G. (2013). Treating obsessive-compulsive disorder in intimate relationships: A pilot study of couple-based cognitive-behavior therapy. Behavior Therapy, 44(3), 395-407. doi: 10.1016/j.beth.2013.02.005

Acitelli, L. K., Douvan, E., & Veroff, J. (1993). Perceptions of conflict in the first year of marriage: How important are similarity and understanding? Journal of Social and Personal Relationships, 10(1), 5-19. https://doi.org/10.1177/0265407593101001

Adams, J. S. (1965). Inequity in social exchange. Advances in Experimental Social Psychology, 2, 267-299. doi: 10.1016/S0065-2601(08)60108-2

Allen, E. S., Atkins, D. C., Baucom, D. H., Snyder, D. K., Gordon, K. C., & Glass, S. P. (2005). Intrapersonal, interpersonal, and contextual factors in engaging in and responding to extramarital involvement. Clinical Psychology: Science and Practice, 12(2), 101-130.

Amato, P. R., & Rogers, S. J. (1997). A longitudinal study of marital problems and subsequent divorce. Journal of Marriage and Family, 59(3), 612-624. doi: 10.2307/353949

Amato, P. R., Booth, A., Johnson, D. R., & Rogers, S. J. (2007). Alone Together: How Marriage in America is Changing. Harvard University Press.

Amstad, F. T., Meier, L. L., Fasel, U., Elfering, A., & Semmer, N. K. (2011). A meta-analysis of work–family conflict and various outcomes with a special emphasis on cross-domain versus matching-domain relations. Journal of Occupational Health Psychology, 16(2), 151-169. doi: 10.1037/a0022170

Archuleta, K. L., Britt, S. L., Tonn, T. J., & Grable, J. E. (2011). Financial satisfaction and financial stressors in marital satisfaction. Psychological Reports, 108(2), 563-576. doi: 10.2466/07.09.21.PR0.108.2.563-576

Aron, A., Norman, C. C., Aron, E. N., & Lewandowski, G. W. (2002). Shared participation in self-expanding activities: Positive effects on experienced marital quality. Personal Relationships, 9(1), 50-63.

Atkins, D. C., Baucom, D. H., & Jacobson, N. S. (2001). Understanding infidelity: Correlates in a national random sample. Journal of Family Psychology, 15(4), 735.

Beach, S. R. H., & O'Leary, K. D. (1993). Dysphoria and marital discord: Are dysphoric individuals at risk for marital maladjustment? Journal of Marital and Family Therapy, 19(4), 355-368.

Bianchi, S. M., Milkie, M. A., Sayer, L. C., & Robinson, J. P. (2000). Is anyone doing the housework? Trends in the gender division of household labor. Social Forces, 79(1), 191-228.

Birditt, K. S., Wan, W. H., Orbuch, T. L., & Antonucci, T. C. (2017). The development of marital tension: Implications for divorce among married couples. Developmental Psychology, 53(10), 1995–2006. doi: 10.1037/dev0000369

Blandon, A. Y., Calkins, S. D., Keane, S. P., & O'Brien, M. (2008). Individual differences in trajectories of emotion regulation processes: The effects of maternal depressive symptomatology and children's physiological regulation. Developmental Psychology, 44(4), 1110-1123. doi: 10.1037/0012-1649.44.4.1110

Bodenmann, G., Bradbury, T. N., & Pihet, S. (2009). Relative contributions of treatment-related changes in communication skills and dyadic coping skills to the longitudinal course of marriage in the framework of marital distress prevention. Journal of Divorce & Remarriage, 50(1), 1-21.

Bodenmann, G., Ledermann, T., & Bradbury, T. N. (2007). Stress, sex, and satisfaction in marriage. Personal Relationships, 14(4), 551–569.

Bodenmann, G., Meuwly, N., & Kayser, K. (2011). Two conceptualizations of dyadic coping and their potential for predicting relationship quality and individual well-being. European Psychologist, 16(4), 255-266.

Bodenmann, G., Plancherel, B., Beach, S. R. H., Widmer, K., & Gabriel, B. (2008). Effects of coping-oriented couples therapy on depression: A randomized clinical trial. Journal of Consulting and Clinical Psychology, 76(6), 944-954.

Bottke, A. (2008). Setting Boundaries® with Your Adult Children: Six Steps to Hope and Healing for Struggling Parents. Harvest House Publishers.

Boxell, L., Gentzkow, M., & Shapiro, J. M. (2020). Cross-country trends in affective polarization. American Political Science Review, 114(2), 413-429.

Brackett, M. A., Rivers, S. E., & Salovey, P. (2011). Emotional intelligence: Implications for personal, social, academic, and workplace success. Social and Personality Psychology Compass, 5(1), 88-103.

Brackett, M. A., Warner, R. M., & Bosco, J. S. (2005). Emotional intelligence and relationship quality among couples. Personal Relationships, 12(2), 197-212.

Bradbury, T. N., & Lavner, J. A. (2012). How can we improve preventive and educational interventions for intimate relationships? Behavior Therapy, 43(1), 113-122.

Bradbury, T. N., Fincham, F. D., & Beach, S. R. (2000). Research on the nature and determinants of marital satisfaction: A decade in review. Journal of Marriage and Family, 62(4), 964-980. doi: 10.1111/j.1741-3737.2000.00964.x

Bradford, A. B., Burningham, K. L., Sandberg, J. G., & Johnson, L. N. (2017). The association between couples' attachment security, intimacy behaviors, and sexual satisfaction. Journal of Marital and Family Therapy, 43(1), 138-150.

Britt, S. L., Cumbie, J. A., & Bell, M. M. (2013). The influence of locus of control on student financial behavior. College Student Journal, 47(1), 178-184.

Britt, S., Hill, E. J., & Tibbetts, R. (2016). The impact of money scripts on marital satisfaction. Journal of Family and Economic Issues, 37(2), 299-313. doi: 10.1007/s10834-015-9445-4

Brownell, J. (1990). Perceptions of effective listeners: A management study. Journal of Business Communication, 27(4), 401-415. doi: 10.1177/002194369002700405

Butler, M. H., & Seedall, R. B. (2010). Therapeutic presence in emotionally focused couples therapy practices that transform. Journal of Marital and Family Therapy, 36(1), 5-18. doi: 10.1111/j.1752-0606.2009.00175.x

Byers, E. S. (2005). Relationship satisfaction and sexual satisfaction: A longitudinal study of individuals in long-term relationships. Journal of Sex Research, 42(2), 113-118.

Carstensen, L. L., Graff, J., Levenson, R. W., & Gottman, J. M. (1996). Affect in intimate relationships: The developmental course of marriage. Journal of Consulting and Clinical Psychology, 64(2), 223-234. doi: 10.1037/0022-006X.64.2.223

Christensen, A., Atkins, D. C., Berns, S., Wheeler, J., Baucom, D. H., & Simpson, L. E. (2004). Traditional versus integrative behavioral couple therapy for significantly and chronically distressed married couples.

Chung, H. (2007). Socio-cultural dimensions of conflicts in interracial and intercultural marriages. The Family Journal, 15(3), 227-239. doi: 10.1177/1066480707301290

Clark, S. C. (2000). Work/family border theory: A new theory of work/family balance. Human Relations, 53(6), 747-770.

Coltrane, S. (2000). Research on household labor: Modeling and measuring the social embeddedness of routine family work. Journal of Marriage and Family, 62(4), 1208-1233.

Conger, R. D., Conger, K. J., & Martin, M. J. (2010). Socioeconomic status, family processes, and individual development. Journal of Marriage and Family, 72(3), 685-704. doi: 10.1111/j.1741-3737.2010.00725.x

Cordova, J. V., Gee, C. B., & Warren, L. Z. (2005). Emotional skillfulness in marriage: Intimacy as a mediator of the relationship between emotional skillfulness and marital satisfaction. Journal of Social and Clinical Psychology, 24(2), 218-235.

Cowan, P. A., & Cowan, C. P. (2000). When partners become parents: The big life change for couples. Lawrence Erlbaum Associates Publishers.

Coyne, J. C., Thompson, R., & Palmer, S. C. (2002). Marital quality, coping with conflict, marital complaints, and affection in couples with a depressed wife. Journal of Family Psychology, 16(1), 26-37.

Cramer, D. (2004). Emotional support, conflict, depression, and relationship satisfaction in a romantic partner. The Journal of Psychology, 138(6), 532-542.

Crawford, D. W., Houts, R. M., Huston, T. L., & George, L. J. (2002). Compatibility, leisure, and satisfaction in marital relationships. Journal of Marriage and Family, 64(2), 433-449.

Curran, M. A., Hazen, N., Jacobvitz, D., & Feldman, A. F. (2005). Representations of early family relationships predict marital maintenance during the transition to parenthood. Journal of Family Psychology, 19(2), 189-197.

Dakin, J., & Wampler, R. (2008). Money does not buy happiness, but it helps: Marital satisfaction, psychological distress, and demographic differences between low- and middle-income clinic couples. American Journal of Family Therapy, 36(4), 300-311. doi: 10.1080/01926180701647412

Dearing, R. L., Stuewig, J., & Tangney, J. P. (2005). On the importance of distinguishing shame from guilt: Relations to problematic alcohol and drug use. Addictive Behaviors, 30(7), 1392-1404. doi: 10.1016/j.addbeh.2005.02.002

Dew, J., & Dakin, J. (2011). Financial disagreements and marital conflict tactics. Journal of Financial Therapy, 2(1), 23-42. doi: 10.4148/jft.v2i1.1414

Dew, J., Britt, S., & Huston, S. (2012). Examining the relationship between financial issues and divorce. Family Relations, 61(4), 615-628.

Doherty, W. J., & Ryder, R. G. (2016). The work–family balance: An analysis of work–family conflict and work–family synergy. Family Relations, 65(1), 7-20.

Donnelly, R. (2016). Financial strain and marital discord: The importance of communication and support. Journal of Family Studies, 24(1), 58-70. doi: 10.1080/13229400.2016.1187656

Donoho, C. J., Crimmins, E. M., & Seeman, T. E. (2013). Marital quality, gender, and markers of inflammation in the MIDUS cohort. Journal of Marriage and Family, 75(1), 127-141.

Doss, B. D., Rhoades, G. K., Stanley, S. M., & Markman, H. J. (2009). The effect of the transition to parenthood on relationship quality: An 8-year prospective study. Journal of Personality and Social Psychology, 96(3), 601-619. doi: 10.1037/a0013969

Doss, B. D., Simpson, L. E., & Christensen, A. (2004). Why do couples seek marital therapy? Professional Psychology: Research and Practice, 35(6), 608-614. doi: 10.1037/0735-7028.35.6.608

Doweiko, H. E. (2011). Concepts of chemical dependency. Brooks/Cole.

Driver, J. L., & Gottman, J. M. (2004). Daily marital interactions and positive affect during marital conflict among newlywed couples. Family Process, 43(3), 301-314. doi: 10.1111/j.1545-5300.2004.00024.x

Duncan, L. G., Coatsworth, J. D., & Greenberg, M. T. (2009). A model of mindful parenting: Implications for parent–child relationships and prevention research. Clinical Child and Family Psychology Review, 12(3), 255-270.

Eagly, A. H., Wood, W., & Diekman, A. B. (2000). Social role theory of sex differences and similarities: A current appraisal. The Developmental Social Psychology of Gender, 123-174.

Eby, L. T., Casper, W. J., Lockwood, A., Bordeaux, C., & Brinley, A. (2005). Work and family research in IO/OB: Content analysis and review of the literature (1980–2002). Journal of Vocational Behavior, 66(1), 124-197. doi: 10.1016/j.jvb.2003.11.003

Eiden, R. D., Lessard, J., Colder, C. R., Livingston, J., Casey, M., & Leonard, K. E. (2019). Developmental cascade model for adolescent substance use from infancy to late adolescence. Developmental Psychology, 55(10), 2149.

Evans, J. St. B. T., & Stanovich, K. E. (2013). Dual-process theories of higher cognition advancing the debate. Perspectives on Psychological Science, 8(3), 223–241. https://doi.org/10.1177/1745691612460685

Falconier, M. K., Jackson, J. B., Hilpert, P., & Bodenmann, G. (2015). Dyadic coping and relationship satisfaction: A meta-analysis. Clinical Psychology Review, 42, 28–46.

Fals-Stewart, W., Birchler, G. R., & O'Farrell, T. J. (1996). Behavioral couples therapy for male substance-abusing patients: Effects on relationship adjustment and drug-using behavior. Journal of Consulting and Clinical Psychology, 64(5), 959-972. doi: 10.1037/0022-006X.64.5.959

Farver, J. A., Narang, S. K., & Bhadha, B. R. (2002). East meets West: Ethnic identity, acculturation, and conflict in Asian Indian families. Journal of Family Psychology, 16(3), 338-350.

Feeney, B. C., & Collins, N. L. (2015). A new look at social support: A theoretical perspective on thriving through relationships. Personality and Social Psychology Review, 19(2), 113-147.

Feeney, J. A., Noller, P., & Callan, V. J. (1994). Attachment style, communication, and satisfaction in the early years of marriage. Advances in Personal Relationships, 5, 269-308.

Feldman, R. (2012). Oxytocin and social affiliation in humans. Hormones and Behavior, 61(3), 380-391.

Fergusson, D. M., Boden, J. M., & Horwood, L. J. (2008). Exposure to childhood sexual and physical abuse and adjustment in early adulthood. Child Abuse & Neglect, 32(6), 607–619. https://doi.org/10.1016/j.chiabu.2006.12.018

Field, T. (2010). Touch for socioemotional and physical well-being: A review. Developmental Review, 30(4), 367-383.

Fincham, F. D., & Linfield, K. J. (1997). A new look at marital quality: Can spouses feel positive and negative about their marriage? Journal of Family Psychology, 11(4), 489-502. doi: 10.1037/0893-3200.11.4.489

Fincham, F. D., Beach, S. R., Harold, G. T., & Osborne, L. N. (1997). Marital satisfaction and depression: Different causal relationships for men and women? Psychological Science, 8(5), 351-357. doi: 10.1111/j.1467-9280.1997.tb00424.x

Fincham, F. D., Stanley, S. M., & Beach, S. R. H. (2007). Transformative processes in marriage: An analysis of emerging trends. Journal of Marriage and Family, 69(2), 275-292.

Fingerman, K. L. (2001). Aging mothers and their adult daughters: A study in mixed emotions. Journal of Marriage and Family, 63(3), 687-698. doi: 10.1111/j.1741-3737.2001.00687.x

Finkel, E. J., Eastwick, P. W., & Reis, H. T. (2015). Best research practices in psychology: Illustrating epistemological and pragmatic considerations with the case of relationship science. Journal of Personality and Social Psychology, 108(2), 275–297. https://doi.org/10.1037/pspi0000007

Finkel, E. J., Hui, C. M., Carswell, K. L., & Larson, G. M. (2014). The suffocation of marriage: Climbing Mount Maslow without enough oxygen. Psychological Inquiry, 25(1), 1-41.

Finkel, E. J., Simpson, J. A., & Eastwick, P. W. (2016). The psychology of close relationships: Fourteen core principles. Annual Review of Psychology, 69, 383-411.

Fiske, S. T., & Taylor, S. E. (2013). Social cognition: From brains to culture. Sage.

Follingstad, D. R., Bradley, R. G., Helff, C. M., & Laughlin, J. E. (2019). A critical examination of the role of alcohol in partner violence perpetration and victimization. Aggressive Behavior, 45(4), 430-446.

Frone, M. R., Russell, M., & Cooper, M. L. (1992). Antecedents and outcomes of work-family conflict: Testing a model of the work-family interface. Journal of Applied Psychology, 77(1), 65-78. doi: 10.1037/0021-9010.77.1.65

Fulmer, C. A., & Gelfand, M. J. (2012). At what level (and in whom) we trust: Trust across multiple organizational levels. Journal of Management, 38(4), 1167-1230.

Gable, S. L., Reis, H. T., Impett, E. A., & Asher, E. R. (2004). What do you do when things go right? The intrapersonal and interpersonal benefits of sharing positive events. Journal of Personality and Social Psychology, 87(2), 228-245. doi: 10.1037/0022-3514.87.2.228

Gager, C. T., & Sanchez, L. (2003). Two as one? Couples' perceptions of time spent together, marital quality, and the risk of divorce. Journal of Family Issues, 24(1), 21-50.

Gawronski, B. (2004). Theory-based bias correction in dispositional inference: The fundamental attribution error is dead, long live the correspondence bias. European Review of Social Psychology, 15(1), 183-217. https://doi.org/10.1080/10463280440000026

Gordon, K. C., Baucom, D. H., & Snyder, D. K. (2004). An integrative intervention for promoting recovery from extramarital affairs. Journal of Marital and Family Therapy, 30(2), 213-231.

Gottman, J. M. (1994). What predicts divorce?: The relationship between marital processes and marital outcomes. Hillsdale, NJ: Lawrence Erlbaum Associates.

Gottman, J. M., & Levenson, R. W. (1992). Marital processes predictive of later dissolution: behavior, physiology, and health. Journal of Personality and Social Psychology, 63(2), 221.

Gottman, J. M., & Levenson, R. W. (1999). What predicts change in marital interaction over time? A study of alternative models. Family Process, 38(2), 143-158. doi: 10.1111/j.1545-5300.1999.00143.x

Gottman, J. M., & Levenson, R. W. (2000). The timing of divorce: Predicting when a couple will divorce over a 14-year period. Journal of Marriage and Family, 62(3), 737-745. doi: 10.1111/j.1741-3737.2000.00737.x

Gottman, J. M., & Levenson, R. W. (2002). A two-factor model for predicting when a couple will divorce: Exploratory analyses using 14-year longitudinal data. Family Process, 41(1), 83-96. https://doi.org/10.1111/j.1545-5300.2002.40102000083.x

Gottman, J. M., & Silver, N. (2015). The seven principles for making marriage work. Harmony.

Greenhaus, J. H., & Beutell, N. J. (1985). Sources of conflict between work and family roles. Academy of Management Review, 10(1), 76-88. doi: 10.5465/amr.1985.4277352

Gurman, A. S., & Fraenkel, P. (2002). The history of couple therapy: A millennial review. Family Process, 41(2), 199-260.

Hahlweg, K., Kaiser, A., Christensen, A., Fehm-Wolfsdorf, G., & Groth, T. (2000). Self-report and observational assessment of couples' conflict: The concordance between the Communication Patterns Questionnaire and the KPI Observation System. Journal of Marriage and the Family, 62, 61–67. doi: 10.1111/j.1741-3737.2000.00061.x

Halford, W. K., Markman, H. J., & Stanley, S. (2008). Strengthening couples' relationships with education: Social policy and public health perspectives. Journal of Family Psychology, 22(4), 497-505.

Hawkins, A. J., & Fackrell, T. A. (2010). Does relationship and marriage education for lower-income couples work? A meta-analytic study of emerging research. Journal of Couple & Relationship Therapy, 9(2), 181-191.

Hawkins, A. J., Blanchard, V. L., Baldwin, S. A., & Fawcett, E. B. (2008). Does marriage and relationship education work? A meta-analytic study. Journal of Consulting and Clinical Psychology, 76(5), 723-734.

Heavey, C. L., Layne, C., & Christensen, A. (1993). Gender and conflict structure in marital interaction: A replication and extension. Journal of Consulting and Clinical Psychology, 61(1), 16–27. doi: 10.1037/0022-006X.61.1.16

Heiman, J. R., Long, J. S., Smith, S. N., Fisher, W. A., Sand, M. S., & Rosen, R. C. (2011). Sexual satisfaction and relationship happiness in midlife and older couples in five countries. Archives of Sexual Behavior, 40(4), 741–753.

Helms, H. M., Supple, A. J., & Proulx, C. M. (2011). Marital satisfaction and breakups differ across on-line and off-line meeting venues. Proceedings of the National Academy of Sciences, 108(33), 12691-12696. doi: 10.1073/pnas.1101597118

Hendrick, S. S. (1988). A generic measure of relationship satisfaction. Journal of Marriage and the Family, 50, 93-98. http://dx.doi.org/10.2307/352430

Herman, J. L. (1992). Trauma and recovery. BasicBooks.

Hill, E. J., Erickson, J. J., Holmes, E. K., & Ferris, M. (2010). Workplace flexibility, work hours, and work-life conflict: Finding an extra day or two. Journal of Family Psychology, 24(3), 349-358. doi: 10.1037/a0019282

Hill, E. J., Yang, C., Hawkins, A. J., & Ferris, M. (2004). A cross-cultural test of the work–family interface in 48 countries. Journal of Marriage and Family, 66(5), 1300-1316.

Holley, J. W., Sturm, T. L., Levenson, R. W., & Haase, C. M. (2018). Exploring longitudinal dyadic patterns in two-person conversations. Journal of Social and Personal Relationships, 35(4), 433-452.

Holley, S. R., Haase, C. M., & Levenson, R. W. (2013). Age-related changes in demand–withdraw communication behaviors. Journal of Marriage and Family, 75(4), 822-836.

Hoss, L., Richardson, L., Axelrod, A. D., & Cravens Pickens, J. (2023). Clinical Guidelines When Addressing Abuse over Telemental Health. Contemporary Family Therapy.

Huston, T. L., Niehuis, S., & Smith, S. E. (2001). The early marital roots of conjugal distress and divorce. Current Directions in Psychological Science, 10(4), 116-119. doi: 10.1111/1467-8721.00129

Impett, E. A., Strachman, A., Finkel, E. J., & Gable, S. L. (2008). Maintaining sexual desire in intimate relationships: The importance of approach goals. Journal of Personality and Social Psychology, 94(5), 808-823. doi: 10.1037/0022-3514.94.5.808

Iyengar, S., Sood, G., & Lelkes, Y. (2012). Affect, not ideology: A social identity perspective on polarization. Public Opinion Quarterly, 76(3), 405-431.

Johnson, D. J. (2007). Transformative cooperation: How individuals and organizations can transform relationships to transform the world. In Cooperrider, D. L., Zandee, D. P., Godwin, L. N., & Avital, M. (Eds.), Organizational Generativity (Vol. 4). Emerald Group Publishing Limited.

Johnson, M. D., Caughlin, J. P., & Huston, T. L. (1999). The tripartite nature of marital commitment: Personal, moral, and structural reasons to stay married. Journal of Marriage and Family, 61(1), 160-177. doi: 10.2307/353891

Johnson, S. M., & Whiffen, V. E. (2003). Made to measure: Adapting emotionally focused couple therapy to partners' attachment styles. Clinical Psychology: Science and Practice, 10(4), 368-381.

Jose, O., Daniel, B. I., & D'Souza, L. A. (2018). Communication and conflict resolution in couples. Journal of Family Psychology, 32(8), 1065-1070.

Julien, D., Chartrand, E., & Bégin, J. (1999). Social networks, structural interdependence, and conjugal adjustment in heterosexual, gay, and lesbian couples. Journal of Marriage and the Family, 61(2), 516-530. doi: 10.2307/353765

Julien, D., Markman, H. J., & Lindahl, K. M. (1989). A comparison of a global and a microanalytic coding system: Implications for future trends in studying interactions. Behavioral Assessment, 11(1), 81-100.

Karney, B. R., & Bradbury, T. N. (1995). The longitudinal course of marital quality and stability: A review of theory, methods, and research. Psychological Bulletin, 118(1), 3-34.

Kellas, J. K., LeClair-Underberg, C., & Normand, E. L. (2018). The role of co-narration in family solidarity: An examination of family group conference transcripts. Journal of Family Communication, 18(3), 204-220.

Keller, P. S., Cummings, E. M., Davies, P. T., & Mitchell, P. M. (2008). Longitudinal relations between parental drinking problems, family functioning, and child adjustment. Development and Psychopathology, 20(1), 195-212. doi: 10.1017/S0954579408000096

Kelley, M. L., & D'Lima, G. M. (2011). Alcohol use and related problems among college student-athletes: Comparing intercollegiate, club, and intramural participants. Journal of College Student Development, 52(5), 507-516.

Kelly, J. F., & Hoeppner, B. (2013). Does Alcoholics Anonymous work differently for men and women? A moderated multiple-mediation analysis in a large clinical sample. Drug and Alcohol Dependence, 130(1-3), 186-193.

Kelly, J. F., Magill, M., & Stout, R. L. (2009). How do people recover from alcohol dependence? A systematic review of the research on mechanisms of behavior change in Alcoholics Anonymous. Addiction Research & Theory, 17(3), 236-259. doi: 10.1080/16066350902770458

Kelly, J. F., Stout, R. L., Magill, M., & Tonigan, J. S. (2011). The role of Alcoholics Anonymous in mobilizing adaptive social network changes: A prospective lagged mediational analysis. Drug and Alcohol Dependence, 114(2-3), 119-126. doi: 10.1016/j.drugalcdep.2010.09.009

Kenney, C. T. (2006). The power of the purse: Allocative systems and inequality in couple households. Gender & Society, 20(3), 354-381.

Kessler, R. C., Chiu, W. T., Demler, O., & Walters, E. E. (2005). Prevalence, severity, and comorbidity of twelve-month DSM-IV disorders in the National Comorbidity Survey Replication (NCS-R). Archives of General Psychiatry, 62(6), 617-627.

Killewald, A. (2016). Money, work, and marital stability: Assessing change in the gendered determinants of divorce. American Sociological Review, 81(4), 696–719. https://doi.org/10.1177/0003122416653112

Kim, J., & Garman, E. T. (2004). Financial stress, pay satisfaction and workplace performance. Compensation & Benefits Review, 36(1), 69-76.

Kluwer, E. S., & Johnson, M. D. (2007). Conflict frequency and relationship quality across the transition to parenthood. Journal of Marriage and Family, 69(5), 1089-1106. doi: 10.1111/j.1741-3737.2007.00434.x

Knee, C. R., Lonsbary, C., Canevello, A., & Patrick, H. (2005). Self-determination and conflict in romantic relationships. Journal of Personality and Social Psychology, 89(2), 997.

Knoester, C., & Eggebeen, D. J. (2006). The effects of the transition to parenthood and subsequent children on men's well-being and social participation. Journal of Family Issues, 27(11), 1532-1560. doi: 10.1177/0192513X06290802

Kornrich, S., Brines, J., & Leupp, K. (2013). Egalitarianism, Housework, and Sexual Frequency in Marriage. American Sociological Review, 78(1), 26-50. doi: 10.1177/0003122412472340

Kossek, E. E., Noe, R. A., & DeMarr, B. J. (1999). Work-family role synthesis: Individual and organizational determinants. International Journal of Conflict Management, 10(2), 102-129. doi: 10.1108/eb022820

Kotov, R. I., Gamez, W., Schmidt, F., & Watson, D. (2017). Linking "big" personality traits to anxiety, depressive, and substance use disorders: a meta-analysis. Psychological bulletin, 143(9), 950.

Lam, D. H., Donaldson, C., Brown, Y., & Malliaris, Y. (2005). Burden and marital and sexual satisfaction in the partners of bipolar patients. Bipolar Disorders, 7(5), 431-440. doi: 10.1111/j.1399-5618.2005.00240.x

Langer, S. L., Brown, J. D., & Syrjala, K. L. (2009). Intrapersonal and interpersonal consequences of protective buffering among cancer patients and caregivers. Cancer, 115(S18), 4311-4325. doi:10.1002/cncr.24586.

Lauer, R. H., Lauer, J. C., & Kerr, S. T. (1990). The long-term marriage: Perceptions of stability and satisfaction. International Journal of Aging and Human Development, 31(3), 189-195. doi: 10.2190/7PNT-3E1L-5URD-R3H8

Laurenceau, J., Barrett, L. F., & Pietromonaco, P. R. (1998). Intimacy as an interpersonal process: The importance of self-disclosure, partner disclosure, and perceived partner responsiveness in interpersonal exchanges. Journal of Personality and Social Psychology, 74(5), 1238–1251. doi: 10.1037/0022-3514.74.5.1238

Lavner, J. A., Karney, B. R., & Bradbury, T. N. (2016). Does couples' communication predict marital satisfaction, or does marital satisfaction predict communication? Journal of Marriage and Family, 78(3), 680-694.

Lawrence, E., Rothman, A. D., Cobb, R. J., Rothman, M. T., & Bradbury, T. N. (2008). Marital satisfaction across the transition to parenthood. Journal of Family Psychology, 22(1), 41-50. doi: 10.1037/0893-3200.22.1.41

Le, B., Dove, N. L., Agnew, C. R., Korn, M. S., & Mutso, A. A. (2010). Predicting nonmarital romantic relationship dissolution: A meta-analytic synthesis. Personal Relationships, 17(3), 377-390.

Lebow, J. L., Chambers, A. L., Christensen, A., & Johnson, S. M. (2012). Research on the treatment of couple distress. Journal of Marital and Family Therapy, 38(1), 145-168.

Leeker, O. Z., & Carlozzi, A. F. (2014). Effects of sex, sexual orientation, infidelity expectations, and love on distress related to emotional and sexual infidelity. Journal of Marital and Family Therapy, 40(1), 68-91. doi: 10.1111/j.1752-0606.2012.00328.x

Leonard, K. E., & Eiden, R. D. (2007). Marital and family processes in the context of alcohol use and alcohol disorders. Annual Review of Clinical Psychology, 3, 285-310.

Lewicki, R. J., Tomlinson, E. C., & Gillespie, N. (2006). Models of interpersonal trust development: Theoretical approaches, empirical evidence, and future directions. Journal of Management, 32(6), 991-1022.

Litzinger, S., & Gordon, K. C. (2005). Exploring relationships among communication, sexual satisfaction, and marital satisfaction. Journal of Sex & Marital Therapy, 31(5), 409-424.

Long, E. C., Angera, J. J., Carter, S. J., Nakamoto, M., & Kalso, M. (1999). Understanding the one you love: A longitudinal assessment of an empathy training program for couples in romantic relationships. Family Relations, 48(3), 235-242.

Lusardi, A., & Mitchell, O. S. (2014). The economic importance of financial literacy: Theory and evidence. Journal of Economic Literature, 52(1), 5-44.

MacNeil, S., & Byers, E. S. (2005). Dyadic assessment of sexual self-disclosure and sexual satisfaction in heterosexual dating couples. Journal of Social and Personal Relationships, 22(2), 169–181. doi: 10.1177/0265407505050942

Mahoney, A., Pargament, K. I., Murray-Swank, A., & Murray-Swank, N. (1999). Religion and the sanctification of family relationships. Review of Religious Research, 40(3), 220-236. doi: 10.2307/3512172

Mäkelä, P. (2004). Studies of the reliability and validity of the Addiction Severity Index. Addiction, 99(4), 398-410. doi: 10.1111/j.1360-0443.2003.00665.x

Malouff, J. M., Schutte, N. S., & Thorsteinsson, E. B. (2014). Trait emotional intelligence and romantic relationship satisfaction: A meta-analysis. The American Journal of Family Therapy, 42(1), 53-66.

Mark, K. P., Janssen, E., & Milhausen, R. R. (2011). Infidelity in heterosexual couples: demographic, interpersonal, and personality-related predictors of extradyadic sex. Archives of Sexual Behavior, 40(5), 971-982.

Mark, K. P., Laurenceau, J. P., & Gonzaga, G. C. (2018). Touch, intimacy, and health among romantic couples. Current Opinion in Psychology, 25, 105-109. doi: 10.1016/j.copsyc.2018.02.025

Markman, H. J., & Rhoades, G. K. (2012). Relationship education research: Current status and future directions. Journal of Marital and Family Therapy, 38(1), 169–200.

Markman, H. J., Stanley, S. M., & Blumberg, S. L. (2010). Fighting for your marriage. Jossey-Bass.

Matthews, L. S., Conger, R. D., & Wickrama, K. A. (1996). Work-family conflict and marital quality: Mediating processes. Social Psychology Quarterly, 39-54.

McCrady, B. S., Epstein, E. E., Cook, S., Jensen, N. K., & Ladd, B. O. (2009). What do women want? Alcohol treatment choices, treatment entry and retention. Psychology of Addictive Behaviors, 23(3), 537-549. doi: 10.1037/a0016587

McKay, J. R. (2017). Treating substance use disorders with adaptive continuing care. American Psychological Association.

McNulty, J. K., Olson, M. A., Meltzer, A. L., & Shaffer, M. J. (2013). Though they may be unaware, newlyweds implicitly know whether their marriage will be satisfying. Science, 342(6162), 1119-1120. https://doi.org/10.1126/science.1243140

Mikulincer, M., & Shaver, P. R. (2007). Attachment in adulthood: Structure, dynamics, and change. New York, NY, US: Guilford Press.

Mikulincer, M., Shaver, P. R., & Pereg, D. (2003). Attachment theory and affect regulation: The dynamics, development, and cognitive consequences of attachment-related strategies. Motivation and Emotion, 27(2), 77-102.

Monson, C. M., Taft, C. T., & Fredman, S. J. (2009). Military-related PTSD and intimate relationships: From description to theory-driven research and intervention development. Clinical Psychology Review, 29(8), 707-714. doi: 10.1016/j.cpr.2009.09.002

Munsch, C. L. (2015). Her support, his support: Money, masculinity, and marital infidelity. American Sociological Review, 80(3), 469-495. https://doi.org/10.1177/0003122415579989

Munsch, C., Perales, F., & Baxter, J. (2020). Gender, Money, and Couple Conflict: A Cross-National Study. Journal of Marriage and Family, 82(1), 324–341.

Neff, L. A., & Karney, B. R. (2004). How does context affect intimate relationships? Linking external stress and cognitive processes within marriage. Personality and Social Psychology Bulletin, 30(2), 134-148. doi: 10.1177/0146167203255984

Neff, L. A., & Karney, B. R. (2017). Acknowledging the elephant in the room: How stressful environmental contexts shape relationship dynamics. Current Opinion in Psychology, 13, 107-110.

Netemeyer, R. G., Boles, J. S., & McMurrian, R. (1996). Development and validation of work–family conflict and family–work conflict scales. Journal of Applied Psychology, 81(4), 400-410. doi: 10.1037/0021-9010.81.4.400

Nichols, R. G., & Stevens, L. A. (1957). Are you listening? McGraw-Hill.

Nomaguchi, K. M. (2009). Change in work-family conflict among employed parents between 1977 and 1997. Journal of Marriage and Family, 71(1), 15-32. doi: 10.1111/j.1741-3737.2008.00577.x

Nomaguchi, K. M. (2012). Parenthood and psychological well-being: Clarifying the role of child age and parent-child relationship quality. Social Science Research, 41(2), 489-498.

Nomaguchi, K. M., & Milkie, M. A. (2003). Costs and rewards of children: The effects of becoming a parent on adults' lives. Journal of Marriage and Family, 65(2), 356-374. doi: 10.1111/j.1741-3737.2003.00356.x

Nowinski, J. (2010). The 12-step facilitation outpatient protocol. Project Match Monograph Series, 1.

O'Farrell, T. J., & Fals-Stewart, W. (2000). Behavioral couples therapy for alcoholism and drug abuse. Journal of Substance Abuse Treatment, 18(1), 51-54. doi:10.1016/S0740-5472(99)00086-8

O'Farrell, T. J., Fals-Stewart, W., & Murphy, M. (2003). Concurrent validity of a brief self-report drug use frequency measure. Addictive Behaviors, 28(2), 327-337. doi: 10.1016/S0306-4603(01)00230-2

O'Farrell, T. J., Murphy, C. M., Stephan, S. H., Fals-Stewart, W., & Murphy, M. (2004). Partner violence before and after couples-based alcoholism treatment for male alcoholic patients: The role of treatment involvement and abstinence. Journal of Consulting and Clinical Psychology, 72(2), 202-217. doi: 10.1037/0022-006X.72.2.202

Osorio Guzmán, M., Prado Romero, C., Morales Navarro, M., Maldonado, H., Carozzo Campos, J. C., Benites Morales, L., & Peralta, P. (2021). Intercultural Latin American research on abuse in couple relationships of young university. Interamerican Journal of Psychology, 55(3).

Paleari, F. G., Regalia, C., & Fincham, F. (2003). Marital quality, forgiveness, empathy, and rumination: A longitudinal analysis. Personality and Social Psychology Bulletin, 29(3), 337-348. doi: 10.1177/0146167202250718

Papp, L. M., Cummings, E. M., & Goeke-Morey, M. C. (2002). Marital conflicts in the home when children are present versus absent. Developmental Psychology, 38(5), 774-783.

Papp, L. M., Cummings, E. M., & Goeke-Morey, M. C. (2009). For richer, for poorer: Money as a topic of marital conflict in the home. Family Relations, 58(1), 91-103.

Pietromonaco, P. R., Uchino, B., & Dunkel Schetter, C. (2013). Close relationship processes and health: Implications of attachment theory for health and disease. Health Psychology, 32(5), 499.

Proulx, C. M., Helms, H. M., & Buehler, C. (2007). Marital quality and personal well-being: A meta-analysis. Journal of Marriage and Family, 69(3), 576-593.

Pulerwitz, J., Amaro, H., De Jong, W., Gortmaker, S. L., & Rudd, R. (2002). Relationship power, condom use and HIV risk among women in the USA. AIDS Care, 14(6), 789–800. doi: 10.1080/09540120210000031868

Randall, A. K., & Bodenmann, G. (2009). The role of stress on close relationships and marital satisfaction. Clinical psychology review, 29(2), 105-115. doi: 10.1016/j.cpr.2008.10.004

Rehman, U. S., Rellini, A. H., & Fallis, E. (2011). The importance of sexual self-disclosure to sexual satisfaction and functioning in committed relationships. Journal of Sexual Medicine, 8(11), 3108-3115. doi: 10.1111/j.1743-6109.2011.02439.x

Reis, H. T., & Shaver, P. R. (1988). Intimacy as an interpersonal process. In S. Duck (Ed.), Handbook of personal relationships: Theory, research and interventions (pp. 367-389). Chichester, England: Wiley.

Reissman, C., Aron, A., & Bergen, M. R. (1993). Shared activities and marital satisfaction: Causal direction and self-expansion versus boredom. Journal of Social and Personal Relationships, 10(2), 243-254.

Repetti, R. L., Taylor, S. E., & Seeman, T. E. (2002). Risky families: family social environments and the mental and physical health of offspring. Psychological Bulletin, 128(2), 330–366. https://doi.org/10.1037//0033-2909.128.2.330

Rhoades, G. K., Stanley, S. M., & Markman, H. J. (2012). The impact of the transition to cohabitation on relationship functioning: Cross-sectional and longitudinal findings. Journal of Family Psychology, 26(3), 348-358.Kornrich, S., Brines, J., & Leupp, K. (2013). Egalitarianism, Housework, and Sexual Frequency in Marriage. American Sociological Review, 78(1), 26-50. doi: 10.1177/0003122412472340

Rodriguez, L. M., Neighbors, C., & Knee, C. R. (2014). Problematic alcohol use and marital distress: An interdependence theory perspective. Addiction Research & Theory, 22(4), 294-312. doi: 10.3109/16066359.2013.841890

Rogers, S. J., & May, D. C. (2003). Spillover between marital quality and job satisfaction: Long-term patterns and gender differences. Journal of Marriage and Family, 65(2), 482-495.

Rogge, R. D., Bradbury, T. N., Hahlweg, K., Engl, J., & Thurmaier, F. (2006). Predicting marital distress and dissolution: Refining the two-factor hypothesis. Journal of Family Psychology, 20(1), 156. doi: 10.1037/0893-3200.20.1.156

Rognmo, K., Torvik, F. A., Ask, H., Roysamb, E., & Tambs, K. (2012). Paternal and maternal alcohol abuse and offspring mental distress in the general population: The Nord-Trondelag health study. BMC Public Health, 12(1), 448. doi: 10.1186/1471-2458-12-448

Ruff, S., McComb, J. L., Coker, C. J., & Sprenkle, D. H. (2010). Behavioral couples therapy for the treatment of substance abuse: A substantive and methodological review of O'Farrell, Fals-Stewart, and colleagues' program of research. Family Process, 49(4), 439-456. doi: 10.1111/j.1545-5300.2010.01333.x

Ruppel, E. K., Jenkins, W. J., Griffin, J. L., & Tefertiller, A. C. (2017). "It's like she's texting me from the other room": Understanding motives for text messaging in parent–young adult relationships. Journal of Family Communication, 17(4), 287-299. doi: 10.1080/15267431.2017.1340299

Rusbult, C. E., & Van Lange, P. A. M. (2003). Interdependence, interaction, and relationships. Annual Review of Psychology, 54, 351–375. doi: 10.1146/annurev.psych.54.101601.145059

Rusbult, C. E., Kumashiro, M., Kubacka, K. E., & Finkel, E. J. (2009). "The part of me that you bring out": Ideal similarity and the Michelangelo phenomenon. Journal of Personality and Social Psychology, 96(1), 61-82.

Rusbult, C. E., Martz, J. M., & Agnew, C. R. (1998). The Investment Model Scale: Measuring commitment level, satisfaction level, quality of alternatives, and investment size. Personal Relationships, 5(4), 357-387.

Rusbult, C. E., Verette, J., Whitney, G. A., Slovik, L. F., & Lipkus, I. (1991). Accommodation processes in close relationships: Theory and preliminary empirical evidence. Journal of Personality and Social Psychology, 60(1), 53. doi: 10.1037/0022-3514.60.1.53

Sanders, M. R., Halford, W. K., & Behrens, B. C. (1999). Parental divorce and premarital couple communication. Journal of Family Psychology, 13(1), 60-74. doi: 10.1037/0893-3200.13.1.60

Schutte, N. S., Malouff, J. M., Bobik, C., Coston, T. D., Greeson, C., Jedlicka, C., ... & Wendorf, G. (2001). Emotional intelligence and interpersonal relations. The Journal of Social Psychology, 141(4), 523-536.

Schwartz, C. R. (1994). Earnings inequality and the changing association between spouses' earnings. American Journal of Sociology, 100(2), 282-312.

Seedall, R. B., & Wampler, K. S. (2013). The Role of Client Interactions in Therapist Feedback: A Qualitative Analysis. Journal of Marital and Family Therapy, 39(4), 425-442. doi:10.1111/j.1752-0606.2012.00318.x

Segrin, C., Hanzal, A., Donnerstein, C., Taylor, M., & Domschke, T. J. (2007). Social skills, psychological well-being, and the mediating role of perceived stress. Anxiety, Stress & Coping, 20(3), 321-329.

Siffert, A., & Schwarz, N. (2011). The role of vulnerability in conflict resolution. Journal of Conflict Resolution, 55(6), 919-941. doi: 10.1177/0022002711407584

Sinha, R. (2008). Chronic stress, drug use, and vulnerability to addiction. Annals of the New York Academy of Sciences, 1141(1), 105-130.

Smith, J. P., & Leonard, K. E. (2005). Alcohol dependence and marital aggression: The loss of positive behaviors. Addictive Behaviors, 30(6), 1107-1121. doi: 10.1016/j.addbeh.2004.09.012

Solis, J. M., Shadur, J. M., Burns, A. R., & Hussong, A. M. (2012). Understanding the diverse needs of children whose parents abuse substances. Current Drug Abuse Reviews, 5(2), 135-147.

Sousa, C., Mason, W. A., Herrenkohl, T. I., Prince, D., Herrenkohl, R. C., & Russo, M. J. (2018). Direct and indirect effects of child abuse and environmental stress: A lifecourse perspective on adversity and depressive symptoms. American Journal of Orthopsychiatry, 88(2), 180–188. https://doi.org/10.1037/ort0000255

South, S. C., Krueger, R. F., & Iacono, W. G. (2011). Understanding General and Specific Connections between Psychopathology and Marital Distress: A Model Based Approach. Journal of Abnormal Psychology, 120(4), 935–947. doi: 10.1037/a0025429

South, S. C., Turkheimer, E., & Oltmanns, T. F. (2008). Personality disorder symptoms and marital functioning. Journal of Consulting and Clinical Psychology, 76(5), 769-780. doi: 10.1037/0022-006X.76.5.769

Sprecher, S. (2001). Equity and social exchange in dating couples: Associations with satisfaction, commitment, and stability. Journal of Marriage and Family, 63(3), 599–613. doi: 10.1111/j.1741-3737.2001.00599.x

Sprecher, S., & Hendrick, S. S. (2004). Self-disclosure in intimate relationships: Associations with individual and relationship characteristics over time. Journal of Social and Clinical Psychology, 23(6), 857-877. doi: 10.1521/jscp.23.6.857.54803

Stanley, S. M., Markman, H. J., & Whitton, S. W. (2002). Communication, conflict, and commitment: Insights on the foundations of relationship success from a national survey. Family Process, 41(4), 659-675.

Stanley, S. M., Rhoades, G. K., & Whitton, S. W. (2010). Commitment: Functions, formation, and the securing of romantic attachment. Journal of Family Theory & Review, 2(4), 243-257. doi: 10.1111/j.1756-2589.2010.00060.x

Stanley, S. M., Whitton, S. W., & Markman, H. J. (2004). Maybe I do: Interpersonal commitment and premarital or nonmarital cohabitation. Journal of Family Issues, 25(4), 496-519. doi: 10.1177/0192513X03257797

Stanley, S. M., Whitton, S. W., & Markman, H. J. (2006). Modifying the effect of relationship education on divorce in low-income couples: A randomized control trial. Journal of Family Psychology, 20(4), 685-695.

Sullivan, K. T., Pasch, L. A., Johnson, M. D., & Bradbury, T. N. (2010). Social support, problem solving, and the longitudinal course of newlywed marriage. Journal of Personality and Social Psychology, 98(4), 631-644.

Tarrier, N., & Wykes, T. (2004). Is there evidence that cognitive behaviour therapy is an effective treatment for schizophrenia? A cautious or cautionary tale? Behaviour Research and Therapy, 42(12), 1377-1401. doi: 10.1016/j.brat.2004.06.020

Tichenor, V. (1999). Status and income as gendered resources: The case of marital power. Journal of Marriage and the Family, 61(3), 638-650.

Tsapelas, I., Aron, A., & Orbuch, T. (2009). Marital boredom now predicts less satisfaction 9 years later. Psychological Science, 20(5), 543-545. doi: 10.1111/j.1467-9280.2009.02332.x

Twenge, J. M., & Campbell, W. K. (2018). Media use is linked to lower psychological well-being: Evidence from three datasets. Psychiatric Quarterly, 89(2), 311-331.

Twenge, J. M., Campbell, W. K., & Foster, C. A. (2003). Parenthood and Marital Satisfaction: A Meta-Analytic Review. Journal of Marriage and Family, 65(3), 574-583.

Vogler, C., Lyonette, C., & Wiggins, R. D. (2008). Money, power and spending decisions in intimate relationships. The Sociological Review, 56(1), 117-143. doi: 10.1111/j.1467-954X.2008.00777.x

Voydanoff, P. (2005). Work demands and work-to-family and family-to-work conflict: Direct and indirect relationships. Journal of Family Issues, 26(6), 707-726.

Walsh, F. (2016). Applying a family resilience framework in training, practice, and research: Mastering the art of the possible. Family Process, 55(4), 616-632.

Weger Jr, H., Castle, G. R., & Emmett, M. C. (2010). Active Listening in Peer Interviews: The Influence of Message Paraphrasing on Perceptions of Listening Skill. International Journal of Listening, 24(1), 34-49. doi: 10.1080/10904010903466311

Weger, H., Castle Bell, G., Minei, E. M., & Robinson, M. C. (2014). The relative effectiveness of active listening in initial interactions. International Journal of Listening, 28(1), 13-31. doi: 10.1080/10904018.2013.813234

Weiss, R. L. (1975). Marital separation. New York: Basic Books.

Whisman, M. A. (2001). The association between depression and marital dissatisfaction. In S. R. H. Beach (Ed.), Marital and family processes in depression: A scientific foundation for clinical practice (pp. 3-24). Washington, DC: American Psychological Association. doi: 10.1037/10350-001

Whisman, M. A. (2007). Marital distress and DSM-IV psychiatric disorders in a population-based national survey. Journal of Abnormal Psychology, 116(3), 638-643. doi: 10.1037/0021-843X.116.3.638

Whisman, M. A., Uebelacker, L. A., & Bruce, M. L. (2006). Longitudinal association between marital dissatisfaction and alcohol use disorders in a community sample. Journal of Family Psychology, 20(1), 164-167. doi: 10.1037/0893-3200.20.1.164

Wieselquist, J., Rusbult, C. E., Foster, C. A., & Agnew, C. R. (1999). Commitment, pro-relationship behavior, and trust in close relationships. Journal of Personality and Social Psychology, 77(5), 942–966. doi: 10.1037/0022-3514.77.5.942

Wymbs, B. T., Pelham, W. E., Molina, B. S., Gnagy, E. M., Wilson, T. K., & Greenhouse, J. B. (2008). Rate and predictors of divorce among parents of youths with ADHD. Journal of Consulting and Clinical Psychology, 76(5), 735-744. doi: 10.1037/a0012719

Zarshenas, L., Baneshi, M., Sharif, F., & Moghimi Sarani, E. (2017). Anger management in substance abuse based on cognitive behavioral therapy: an interventional study. BMC Psychiatry, 17(1).

Zeidner, M., Matthews, G., & Roberts, R. D. (2012). The emotional intelligence, health, and well-being nexus: What have we learned and what have we missed?. Applied Psychology: Health and Well-Being, 4(1), 1-30.

www.ingramcontent.com/pod-product-compliance
Lightning Source LLC
Chambersburg PA
CBHW060419010526
44118CB00017B/2285